CONTENTS

Introduction	1
1 The Church Without a Pastor	19
2 The Church in Chang Family Village	30
3 Where a Celestial Empire Began	43
4 God at Work in Vanity Fair	54
5 China's "Jerusalem"	65
6 The Church Among the Hill Tribes	76
7 Where Living Waters Flow	89
8 The Church in Big Horse Lane	110
Causes of Church Growth	123
Appendix — Summary of Church Growth Around China	131
Map	132
Bibliography	147

INTRODUCTION

THE TIME WAS early summer — festival time. The narrow streets of Jerusalem were milling with pilgrims who had travelled from all over the Mediterranean region to be present. The babel of languages was like London's Oxford Street in the tourist season. The inns were all full and the eating houses doing a roaring trade. For days, pilgrims in their thousands had been thronging the Temple courts to worship Jehovah, the God of Israel. For most of them, the name of Jesus was but a faint rumour.

The earliest church

In one house in Jerusalem, however, that name was honoured. There the apostles and the women gathered daily to pray in the name of their crucified, risen and ascended Lord. They shared an eager expectation of something remarkable about to happen — they did not quite know what.

On the fiftieth day after the Feast of Firstfruits, a series of dramatic events astounded the company assembled in Mark's spacious family home. The long-promised Holy Spirit was outpoured and the Christian Church was born. Crowds immediately began to gather around Mark's house to hear the apostles from Galilee declaring the mighty acts of God in the different languages spoken by the pilgrims.

Peter at once realized that the time had come to declare the Good News publicly and to explain the significance of what was taking place. Supported by the other eleven apostles, he preached his first world-shaking sermon to the astonished and receptive crowds. Deep conviction and repentance followed and three thousand believers were immediately baptized in one day! What exhilarating, thrilling, God-glorifying days those must have been. New believers continued to be added daily until 5,000 men were believing, not to mention their wives and families.

This was what Roland Allen, missionary to China with the Society for the Propagation of the Gospel at the time of the 1911 Nationalist Revolution, called "The Spontaneous Expansion of the Church". He would have been amazed could he have foreseen events in China eighty years on!

The Temple now became the meeting place for the thousands of new Christians who virtually monopolized the sacred building for their own daily worship. At last it had genuinely become a place of prayer for all nations. Joyful praises resounded around the walls of the city, and the apostles found themselves rushed off their feet from morning to night teaching the new believers and praying with them. The huge problem of catering for such large crowds was simplified by the generous hospitality of the local residents, who opened their homes to all for meals and fellowship.

Initial church growth

Out in the Judean countryside, beneath the hot summer sun, the reapers were gathering in the wheat harvest. In Jerusalem, an even greater harvest was being reaped.

In the parable of the sower and the seed, our Lord made it clear that the preaching of the gospel would not always enjoy guaranteed success under all circumstances. Some seed-sowing, Jesus said, would prove quite fruitless, some disappointing after early promise, while only some seed would produce a harvest of a hundred percent. The parable of the mustard seed also foretold the phenomenal growth of the kingdom of God.

And so it proved, as the gospel spread rapidly through Judea, Samaria, Syria, Asia Minor and over into Europe. There Paul and his colleagues, travelling widely, secured new bases throughout the Roman Empire for ongoing evangelism. The Christian Church inevitably began to challenge the might of that Empire. Christ had seized the power from Caesar!

Growth slows down

Wonderful though this early dramatic growth of the Christian Church was, the spectacular events which accompanied the birth of the Church were not repeated. On the contrary, God's servants the apostles often found the ground for seed-sowing hard — as in Athens. There was also much stony ground, as in Asia Minor. And everywhere they went the Good Seed of God's Word was almost smothered by the thorns and thistles of pagan philosophies and lifestyles.

Athens, the centre of Greek culture, and Rome, the

capital of world power, both presented formidable opposition to the gospel. Strong and even violent opposition also came from Jewish traditionalists. Church growth, confronted with Jewish conservatism, Greek philosophy and Roman authoritarianism, slowed down after the initial burst of life.

Barriers to growth

This pattern of hard ground, stony ground and thorny ground, with only a small percentage of good soil, has continued to characterize the proclamation of the gospel worldwide. The nature of the soil varies from nation to nation and from culture to culture.

Ethnic religions like Islam, Hinduism and Buddhism which become an integral part of the national culture prove formidable barriers to progress. In these situations growth is painfully slow, and sociological theories of church growth have not yet solved this dilemma.

On the other hand, church growth has always been greatest in the animistic, tribal societies of Africa, South America, China and southeast Asia. Here so-called "people's movements" have often resulted in whole villages or tribes being brought within the orbit of the Christian Church. To what extent such mass movements are a good thing for Christianity continues to be a matter for debate.

China's opposition to Christianity

China's response to the gospel illustrates both these factors. On the one hand, the greatest growth was among the animistic tribes of the south west, untouched until recently by Han Chinese culture. On the other hand, the philosophies propounded by "the great sage" Confucius and the mystic Laozi, founder of Daoism, have yielded little ground to Christianity over the centuries. Both religions have profoundly influenced the social life and culture of the Chinese — their art, poetry and architecture.

The Confucian classics used to be the text books for the examinations qualifying scholars for government office. These influential scholars or mandarins were intensely proud of their ancient culture, its high ideals and noble standards of morality, with the special emphasis on family life and loyalty. They scorned what they regarded as inferior foreign religions. These included the idolatrous Buddhism which came from India in the early years of the Christian era, and especially Christianity.

The corrupt Nestorian form of Christianity reached China in the seventh century and Roman Catholicism arrived in the thirteenth and sixteenth centuries. The Protestant Church only gained a foothold as late as 1842 following the British victory over China in the First Opium War. That war and the treaties subsequently imposed on a humiliated China provoked a hatred of all foreigners and their religion. Not only China's scholars but the Chinese people as a whole vigorously and often violently opposed all attempts to spread Christianity in their country.

Church growth in the nineteenth century was, therefore, infinitesimally slow. The antagonism reached a climax in 1900 when thousands of Chinese converts and 188 missionaries were massacred by Boxer soldiers. This event stunned the world.

Missionary endeavour

In the new century missionaries multiplied. They were active not only in evangelism but also in educational and medical work, and social work on behalf of orphans and the handicapped. It was missionaries who pioneered modern education and medicine in China. They established seven excellent universities and set up hundreds of regional hospitals and several first-class medical colleges. K S Latourette, the historian, writes, "Their activities were multitudinous... They founded and maintained some of the best educational institutions in the country. The modern medical and nursing professions owe them their inception and most of their development... They promoted education in public health, helped in relieving famine and aided the study of agricultural problems and methods."

In spite of all this, conversions and baptisms remained proportionately few. When in 1951 the Communist Revolution forced missionaries to withdraw from China, they left behind a mere 700,000 communicant Christians of all denominations in a population of 500 million — not an impressive figure after 110 years of costly missionary endeavour!

The Three Self Patriotic Movement

After the Communist victory in 1949 and during the Land Reform period, the Church was rocked by political campaigns. It was accused of being a tool of imperialism. Many individual leaders suffered humiliation, physical abuse and even death. Only a few churches were permitted to remain open. It appears that Roman Catholics bore the brunt of the government's assault against religion.

In 1950 a group of self-appointed Christian leaders met under the direction of the Religious Affairs Bureau (RAB), an organ of the new Communist government. Missionaries had taught the churches the principles of self-support, self-government and self-propagation. Now this group appropriated the familiar missionary slogan and set in motion the "Three Self Patriotic Movement" (TSPM). Patriotism was emphasized above all, and churches were required to sever their financial and administrative links with "imperialist" organizations based in the USA, Britain and elsewhere. This made it impossible for foreign missionaries to continue their work.

Virtually all missionaries withdrew from China in 1951, handing over their extensive properties to the Chinese government. Roman Catholics were also required to forswear their loyalty to the Pope and to form a "patriotic" Catholic organization independent of the Vatican. Thus the era of foreign missions came to an abrupt end.

But not all Christians were prepared to conform to the new government-controlled organization. Brave individuals like Wang Mingdao of Beijing and Watchman Nee of Shanghai could not accept control, however indirect, from an atheist government. At great personal cost — 15 years imprisonment for Watchman Nee and 22 years exile for Wang Mingdao — these well-known Christian leaders refused to cooperate with the TSPM. And an increasing number of Chinese believers who shared their convictions have followed the same costly pathway.

After the Hundred Flowers campaign in 1956, half a million "intellectuals" who had dared to criticize the new regime were banished to labour camps where they remained for up to 14 years. This included many pastors.

In 1958 the Great Leap Forward experiment with "people's communes" was instituted. Mismanagement and drought resulted in disaster for the experiment and Chairman Mao had to step down from his presidency. Another result was that most church buildings were closed and commandeered for factories or store houses. Christians were therefore forced to meet either in private homes or in the open air. These "family meetings", to use the precise translation of the term, were the origin of the "household church" or "house church" movement in China.

The Cultural Revolution

In 1966, the full fury of the fearful and disastrous "Great Proletarian Cultural Revolution" was forced on the nation by a bitter Chairman Mao. The Church was a prime target. Red Guards, consisting largely of university and high school students, were released from their studies and ran riot throughout China in obedience to Chairman Mao and his Little Red Book.

Few escaped suffering in some form, and most Christians were called to endure terrible persecution. Those church buildings not already closed were confiscated. Bibles and Christian literature were systematically destroyed in huge bonfires which pastors were often required to fuel and witness. Many more families suffered separation, as the men were taken away to labour camps and the young people sent to work on the farms. Chaos prevailed throughout China.

Bibles became so scarce that Christians resorted to

hand-copying those few that had escaped destruction. Where possible, copies were hidden away, sometimes under the wrapping of the Little Red Book.

For six years only rumours about the Church or individual Christians reached the outside world. Officially, Christians no longer existed. Total silence prevailed. Even the government-sponsored TSPM disappeared from view. Had the numerically small and spiritually weak Church survived? This anxious question haunted China's friends and kept the world wondering.

The window opens

In February 1972 US President Richard Nixon paid a surprise visit to China. Premier Zhou Enlai thus opened the windows of China just a little, and the world caught its first glimpse of the terrible events that had brought China to near destruction. Church leaders, it was discovered, had borne the brunt of the persecution. Some had been driven to suicide. Others had been executed on suspicion of association with the Chiang Kai-shek regime or antagonism to the policies of Chairman Mao. Some were to spend many years in prison. The whole Church had suffered greatly, along with the entire nation.

Then China's friends were amazed by a report from Fuzhou, capital city of the province of Fujian (see map on page 133). A church which had sprung up during the recent dreadful years had over 1,000 believers! A few years later Bishop Xie Pinxi of Fuzhou reported 20,000 Christians in that city of one million inhabitants, with thousands more in the countryside. By 1986, large crowds were attending the four city churches, while in the country there were hundreds of "meeting points" —

gatherings without their own place of worship. One visiting tourist found house meetings representing literally thousands of Christians. In some places as many as 500 crowded into one building, all enthusiastic in the Spirit, singing, preaching, testifying and exalting the Name of Jesus.

Something quite extraordinary in the way of church growth had begun in the dark days, and was gathering momentum throughout the whole of Fujian province. There are now 560 "registered" churches and the TSPM has baptized 400,000 new believers since 1982. Before the revolution, this province had a large number of Watchman Nee's "Little Flock" or "Christian Assemblies" — a solid foundation on which to build.

The beginning of growth

In 1976 China's three prominent leaders all died — first Premier Zhou Enlai, then Chairman Mao Zedong, and finally the legendary Marshal Zhu De. The Gang of Four (which included Chairman Mao's widow) who were plotting to seize power were immediately arrested, and the Cultural Revolution came to an abrupt end after ten years of disaster.

Real education had been at a standstill. "Intellectuals", which included scientists, engineers, doctors, teachers and other educated people (the "stinking ninth category" of counter-revolutionaries according to Mao) had been detained in prison. In 1979 the order went out for all intellectuals, including Christian pastors, to be released and rehabilitated.

Some pastors had been in prison for over 20 years. To their amazement they returned to find fast-growing churches and a new and exciting ministry awaiting them. One pastor said, "I worried a great deal about my sheep when I was jailed in the 1950s. I had ministered to three congregations of about 300 people altogether. But when I was released in 1978 I found that they had grown to 20 congregations with a total of 5,000 Christians. By 1985, each congregation had over 1,000 people with a total membership of 20,000!"

Another pastor, when released, moved to a very remote area where the church was small. He saw it grow to over 100,000.

In 1977, for the first time for many years, Christians were able to hold meetings in their homes, to sing hymns and read the Bible without fear of being reported or arrested. In 1980 the first church buildings were restored to Christian use in Shanghai and other coastal cities. Thousands of rejoicing believers attended the opening services. Tourism began to be a major industry, and foreign Christians saw first-hand evidences of the almost incredible church growth. Former missionaries visiting China were warmly greeted by old friends and colleagues who confirmed the reports they had heard.

As the Christian Church recovered from this long period of persecution and repression, it found strength and courage to witness to a nation disillusioned with Maoism and Marxism. Remarkable growth followed during the next decade. People spoke of the Church in China as possibly the fastest growing church in the world.

House churches

The largest church growth has undeniably been in the independent "house churches". These are quite different in origin and character from house churches in the west. China's house churches are found mostly in the rural areas. They are in no way linked. There is no nationwide network connecting them, and no common doctrinal belief. The only unifying factor is a determination to be guided by Holy Scripture. They will continue to be the norm as long as there are insufficient church buildings to accommodate the millions of new believers. The lack of Bibles and Bible teachers means inevitable deviations, but prodigious Chinese memories have retained large portions of Scripture and the words of many hymns, so ensuring the continuity of truth through the illumination of the Holy Spirit.

House churches are strenuously opposed by the TSPM and suspected by the government. Consequently, their leaders face arrest and imprisonment by the Public Security Bureau (PSB), often with the collusion of the TSPM. Since 1989 the government has imposed heavy penalties to force house churches to close down or register with the TSPM.

The house churches largely depend upon the ministry of itinerant evangelists. This is not only because of the shortage of Bibles but also because the large majority of rural people are illiterate or semiliterate.

Almost all these evangelists are volunteers who have to earn their own living. Consequently they face real financial difficulties. For instance, a school teacher who believed and began witnessing was dismissed from his school and sent to work in the fields. He continued preaching there, but was falsely accused and imprisoned for ten years. His wife and three children were left without support, and although his wife was in deep need she refused help from other believers. She felt it was an honour for them to suffer for the Lord in this way.

The movement for democracy

In the winter of 1978-79 the Democracy Wall in Beijing attracted world-wide attention. Dissidents plastered the Wall with "large character posters". These were formerly used during the Cultural Revolution to promote revolution, but now expressed opposition to Maoism and demanded an end to corruption, greater freedom for the individual and for the press, and a change to a truly democratic system of government. Dissident newspapers circulated among the crowds that gathered to read the posters and, for the first time in many years, foreign correspondents mingled with the crowds and talked to the dissidents. Euphoria was in the air, as some hoped changes might be imminent.

This freedom could not last, and Deng Xiaoping eventually brought it to an end. Some of the leading dissidents were arrested, tried and imprisoned. Hu Yaobang, the Party Secretary, showed sympathy with the democracy movement and was consequently popular with the students. His fall from power in 1987 was a severe setback to the movement. However Zhao Ziyang, Hu's successor, continued to support the reform movement.

1989 proved to be a fateful year as the prevailing unrest came to the surface. Pro-democracy demonstrations began in April and took place in three stages. The first followed the death of Hu Yaobang, the students' hero, who was regarded as a martyr to their cause. Banners opposing Deng and Premier Li Peng appeared, and large marches took place demanding democracy, free speech, a free press and the reform of the Party.

Then, to commemorate the May 4th Movement of 1919 — a landmark in China's political history — colleges and universities in 25 other cities staged marches in sympathy with their Beijing fellow-students and were joined by several hundred journalists. Zhao Ziyang expressed his sympathy, holding the view that the students were not involved in a conspiracy but expressing legitimate views about reform.

Tiananmen

During April, Tiananmen Square in Beijing was continuously occupied by 40,000 students, many of whom were on hunger strike. They made their headquarters on the Martyrs' Memorial, and their banners floated constantly over the square. Expectations rose that Deng Xiao-ping and Li Peng would step down and their demands would be met. A leading student activist was invited to meet the government leaders and forcefully berated Li Peng.

It was unfortunate that Soviet leader Gorbachev made a scheduled and potentially important first visit to China just at this time. The students used his visit to call attention to the reforms taking place in the Soviet Union. As he met with Chinese leaders in the Great Hall of the People on the north side of Tiananmen Square, their discussions were almost drowned by the din of more than a million demonstrators outside. This was a grave loss of face for the Chinese leadership.

Martial law was declared, but at first the army refused to act against the people and kept largely out of sight. But the threat of force against the peaceful demonstrators was the only weapon left to the government. Party

Secretary Zhao Ziyang was the only member of the Politburo to dissociate himself from a violent solution. He was immediately stripped of all his posts and Jiang Zemin succeeded him.

The students who had been camping out in Tiananmen Square for weeks were ordered to leave. But they made no move to obey, and the government leaders again lost face. Early in the morning of Sunday June 4 either Deng or Li or both ordered the army to clear the square with whatever force was necessary.

A column of tanks advanced, crushing tents with their occupants. One lone, courageous student stood in front of the column and temporarily halted it. Millions around the world saw this incident on TV. Then the infantry opened fire with machine guns on the defenceless students, leaving hundreds dead[1] and many more severely wounded. Hospitals filled to overflowing. The bodies of the dead were incinerated on the spot by the authorities who refused to admit to the massacre.

A thorough purge followed. By November 80,000 suspected "counter-revolutionaries" had been arrested and as many as 10,000 officials lost their jobs, including leading reformists, academics and newspaper editors. Strict controls were placed on the universities and students were once again submitted to hard-line ideological indoctrination. Tight censorship of the press and stricter restrictions on those wishing to study abroad were imposed. The democracy movement was temporarily crushed.

All this left China's intellectuals profoundly disillusioned with Communism. A spirit of hopelessness per-

[1] Amnesty International say 1300

vaded China, and the underlying unrest and discontent continued. A genuine democracy movement still undoubtedly exists and must ultimately prevail. Dissidents abroad have founded the Federation for a Democratic China with a worldwide membership, though with unclear goals.

The effect on Christians

Among the demonstrators in Tiananmen Square were Christian groups carrying banners with Christian slogans. Bishop K H Ding, chairman of the TSPM, sent a message to the government leaders urging them not to use force against the students and to listen to their complaints, but in vain. Later he was forced to confess his "mistake".

Persecution of Christians followed quickly on the heels of the crackdown on the democracy movement. Seminary students who had taken part in the Tiananmen demonstrations were beaten up by the police, short-wave radios were confiscated from Christian homes, itinerant evangelists found travel more difficult as the new identity card law was enforced, and peasant Christians were warned to replace worship of God with an earnest study of official decrees. Numerous house churches were forced to close, including the one in the home of Pastor Lamb in Guangzhou (see chapter 8), and heavy fines were imposed on a church in Henan.

"Foreign experts", that is professionals in education, business and industry, endured a new attitude of suspicion as to their real motives. Listening to foreign, especially Christian, broadcasts was frowned on. The momentous changes in the USSR and in Eastern Europe since the end of 1989 have alarmed the government. It has applied more pressure on state and house churches, believing that Christianity was a primary cause of the unwelcome changes affecting these former allies.

But have these things halted the growth of the Church in China? Not at all! Thousands have continued to turn to Christ every day. Significantly, these include many educated people such as professors, lecturers and students. Traditional Chinese religions provided no answer to their problems. Thinking people are searching for an alternative philosophy to Marxism and materialism.

Churches have been overwhelmed with the influx of intellectuals whose questions and spiritual needs church leaders are ill-prepared to satisfy. Many such people do not meet in either open or house churches, but in groups seeking to discover the Bible's answers to ideological, social and personal problems. Bible study groups are mushrooming on college campuses everywhere.

In Beijing University, whose student body was decimated on Tiananmen Square, eight students a day were coming to Christ at one time. In December 1990 the hall was packed for the second seminar in a series of four focusing on the Bible and the influence of Christianity. The authorities, alarmed at the interest, suspended the last two lectures. In at least five cities in south China, ten percent of the student body turned to Christ.

In August 1989 a house church pastor in central China called for a nationwide day of prayer for revival and stability. Church growth in Fujian province was such that the national press spoke of "Christian fever."

Three churches in one county were so crowded that the believers petitioned the government for more buildings. And the new surge included many young, educated people. Even in Inner Mongolia, in the month following the crackdown after Tiananmen, one evangelist reported more conversions than in the previous three years.

In January 1990 the government complained that Communist Party membership had decreased during the past three years, while those becoming Christians in the major cities had more than doubled. The Holy Spirit has been powerfully at work in many hearts which were empty with despair, crying out for meaning in life.

This book tells the stories of eight churches or areas that have experienced phenomenal growth in the years since 1979. The identity of the churches and their pastors has in most cases not been disclosed. Even the geographical location is not given precisely, and some of the authors wish to remain anonymous to protect their subjects. But these are true case histories of real churches in which God has been mightily at work.

In Nehemiah's day the wall of the city of God was built under the threats of enemies to attack and disrupt the work. Eternal vigilance was needed. So now the new believers and their leaders in China still face strong and increasing opposition from the great enemy of the Church.

May this record of God's mighty acts in and through His growing Church in China bring glory to His Name alone!

ONE

THE CHURCH WITHOUT A PASTOR

Paul Kauffmann
Founder of Asian Outreach

IT WAS NOT ALWAYS a church without a pastor. Only during its most dramatic growth period.

This story begins after the Communist victory in 1949. Change came fast to China as the Communist Party began to tighten its grip on the churches. But there was still work to be done for Christ.

A young man whom we shall call Pastor Chung felt in his heart a burden for the villages on the east coast of China. For the most part the villagers were very poor, many of them fisherfolk. Pastor Chung, on the other hand, was well-educated and city bred. Nevertheless he felt God calling him to plant a church among these simple village folk.

In 1953 he answered God's call. Leaving the relative comfort and security of his home city he settled among them. Like God's servants through the ages he could never have imagined what lay in the future. All he knew was that he had been called there. Pastor Chung settled to his task and over the next seven years he succeeded in planting a church with three separate meeting points — this made it easier for the widely scattered village people to attend worship and other services. His flock grew to 300 baptized believers, which already represented significant growth at that time.

These were difficult years to plant a church. Evangelical pastors who would not agree to bring their churches under government control were being bullied and publicly denounced. Three times Pastor Chung was detained, publicly humiliated and accused. His crimes: planting a church without official permission, writing and publishing Christian literature, and refusing to join the TSPM. He continued to refuse to conform to government dictates and thereby compromise the people of God.

In 1969 the Communist Party ordered Pastor Chung's arrest and sent him to a labour camp. But before his arrest the church he planted had experienced the power of God. For the purpose of this story and to protect his identity, let us call it the church of Ningchung.

Pastor Chung spent nine years in the labour camp, which included the dreadful years of the Cultural Revolution. All that time he had no contact with the believers in Ningchung. More and more pastors and Christian workers came crowding into the labour camps and he heard from them how during the Cultural Revolution all public expression of church activity had been crushed. With a broken heart he learned that pastors and evangelists had been arrested, all churches closed and all Bibles and other Christian literature confiscated or publicly burned.

Such news drove Pastor Chung to prayer and intercession. He wondered how the Church could possibly survive such a concerted onslaught. No church buildings, no pastors, no Bibles! "Oh God," he cried, "have mercy on your people. Have mercy on China!" Much of his time in internment was spent in prayer, not for himself but for the people of God and for his troubled nation. Even in hard labour, he prayed as he worked, often waist deep in human excrement used to fertilize the fields.

With the death of Chairman Mao and the arrest of the "Gang of Four" in 1976, things began to change. In 1978 Pastor Chung was released, and wasted no time returning to see what had happened in Ningchung. He wondered what he would find. Would there be any believers left?

He first went to the home of one of the key members, hoping that, if he were alive, he would know what had happened to the flock of God. How great was their joy when they recognized the pastor they had not seen or even heard of for nine years! What a time of thanksgiving to God! But what had happened to the church?

Pastor Chung listened with growing joy and amazement as the elder told him how God had not merely preserved His Church, but had multiplied it seventeen times. Pastor Chung discovered that the congregation had grown to 5,000 baptized believers, and this during the most difficult of times.

What was it, besides the faithful prayers of its pastor during his years of internment, that had caused that church to grow so dramatically? Pastor Chung has carefully examined this question, and has identified eight ingredients that God used to bring about growth in the church of Ningchung.

1. Persecution
Persecution forced the Christians to depend wholly

on the Lord because there was no one else to depend on. Virtually all human props were removed. Pastor Chung reminds us that we are all dependent on the Lord, but we tend to think we can get along without Him. In times when every other prop is taken away we are forced to depend on Him alone. In the case of the church in Ningchung, the repeated arrests of the pastor and his final incarceration signalled the beginning of pressure by the government and the TSPM. This reached its peak during the ten years of the Cultural Revolution. God became the church's only dependable refuge, their only unfailing Friend and their inspiration for life. The Christians were thus an attraction to others who had no such recourse. So the church in Ningchung grew in the Lord and in numbers.

2. Prayer

Persecution drove the Ningchung Christians to prayer. They soon found that the safest and best time to gather for prayer was 3 am. As this discovery spread to other groups of believers, 3 am prayer meetings became common in many parts of China. These early morning prayer meetings became the strength of China's church, as had happened in Korea.

Each crisis evoked more prayer. And there were almost daily crises either for individuals or for the church. For instance, during the Cultural Revolution, with no pastors left to hound and persecute, the wrath of the government turned on the known lay leaders, the elders of the church. When the believers discovered that a local elder had been singled out for "criticism", they knew that he was going to be insulted, blamed, demeaned and forced to endure a cruel form of "self-criticism" before the masses, which involved publicly criticizing your own beliefs and even your family. Some broke under the extreme pressure. The church went to prayer at the same hour as the "criticism" meeting was to take place, and as they prayed they grew in grace and inner strength. The elder involved was aware that, while he was being criticized, the church was praying. What a source of strength! He knew also that the church was not praying he would be spared from public demeaning, but that the Lord would give him strength to endure. The church did not pray to avoid suffering, persecution or hardships.

The Christians relied on Scripture to strengthen them in the affliction. As they prayed they quoted such Scriptures as Hebrews 12:11, "No discipline seems pleasant at the time, but painful. Later on, however, it produces a harvest of righteousness and peace for those who have been trained by it."

It soon became common knowledge that the Christians had an inner strength that others did not have. Frequently, non-Christians going through particularly intolerable circumstances would seek out the Christians and ask them to pray for them. Many found the Lord during these times of prayer. And so the church in Ningchung grew.

3. Scripture memorization

Many of China's older generation were illiterate. Such Christians could only feed on God's Word by memorizing it. With the help of a younger person they committed whole chapters to memory. Thus the Scriptures were deeply ingrained in both the young and the old and could not be taken away from them, no matter how hard the authorities tried. And so the church in Ningchung grew.

The Scriptures even became their songbook. I have heard Christians sing as many as ten whole chapters from memory in a single worship session: God's Word ranging from Old to New Testament, from praise to exhortation, from worship to encouragement. The tunes seemed both natural and indigenous. I have never heard singing that so deeply involved the worshippers. God's Word must be the ultimate hymnbook. And so the church in Ningchung grew.

After the government had confiscated or burned all the Bibles they could find, God's Word became even more highly valued. Since new converts could not be given a Bible or even a Scripture portion, older Christians felt a responsibility to help them learn whole chapters by heart. When services were held, even in secret, they tended to be very long. Much time was given to Bible teaching, Scripture memorization and the singing of Scripture. All-day services became commonplace. God's Word held the central place, as it should. And so the church in Ningchung grew.

4. Multiplication of meeting points

This became an absolute necessity for two reasons. At one period all Christian meetings were illegal. So the elders in Ningchung concluded that, in order to escape detection, it would be best to divide the congregation into several meeting points. But as the church continued to grow the leadership had to find additional places where the believers could assemble. As only the homes of believers could be used, sheer numbers forced them to multiply meeting points. And wherever the church met it attracted new believers, and so the church at Ningchung grew.

5. Multiplication of leaders

Virtually all of China's seminary and Bible school trained leaders were incarcerated as "intellectuals" by the sixties. This was the opportunity for the Holy Spirit to raise up new leaders from each local church. The Holy Spirit was faithful. As a result the Church not only had more leaders than before the revolution, but these leaders had only the Bible to guide them. This led to a form of Christianity for which the Early Church was the clear pattern, not some human tradition or ecclesiastical body but the activity of the Holy Spirit in building His Church. The new leaders knew that Jesus Christ was the Head of the true Church. The elders of the rapidly multiplying churches in the country became more and more biblical in their approach to the Church. And so the church in Ningchung grew.

6. Acceptance of the supernatural

Freed from a leadership that might have ruled out the supernatural as part of another dispensation, the believers were in a position to make room for God to work supernaturally. Also, their refusal to accept Communist Party regulations meant they were not bound by the stipulation that the supernatural was taboo. To the leaders of the Party, the miracle-working power of God was anathema.

The government itself set the stage for God to work. The most common form of medicine in China, the ancient herbal tradition and the medicine shops, were condemned as a form of capitalism or private ownership and forced to go out of business. Politically unsatisfactory physicians were banished to labour camps, and doctors who had not been "purged" were ordered into the cities to fill the resulting vacancies. This left the country people, 80% percent of the population, virtually without medical care. Even the witch doctors with their evil practices were driven out of business while the so-called "barefoot doctors" were ill-trained and consequently distrusted.

But people still fell ill! The sick could not walk the 20 or more kilometres to the nearest hospital or clinic; nor could they afford to hire four labourers to carry them that distance. No cars or other forms of transport were available. Only the Christians had access to healing in answer to prayer. News spread fast. Christians prayed to Jesus and He healed!

It is difficult to estimate how many came to Christ for healing and were then led to trust Him as their Saviour, but there is no denying that this was and is a very significant factor in the growth of the church in Ningchung and throughout China. The prayer of faith by ordinary Christians "saved the sick" and the church in Ningchung grew.

Another dimension that contributed to the growth of the church was exorcism. Demonic activity, which has always been prevalent in China with its many traditional animistic practices, is even more pronounced during times of revolution and rebellion. Demon possession was and is a common problem that can only be dealt with by the power of God. The Christians of Ningchung understood this. Often they were the last hope after every other avenue had been tried. Families went from hospitals to secret Buddhist priests to witch doctors. Then, when they had exhausted every other known possibility and had been drained of all their money, word would reach them that the Christian God was more powerful than the evil spirits. And He was indeed. These Christians knew how to exercise authority over all evil spirits in the all-powerful Name of Jesus. And the church in Ningchung grew.

7. A caring church

The believers thought more about the needs of others than their own needs. This was true from the leadership clear through to the individual Christians. The leaders felt responsible for the spiritual well-being of every Christian. During week nights, where possible, key leaders would gather together with their notebooks to share the Scriptures. They learned from one another. Often these leadership meetings were held late at night and lasted until the early morning hours. Even though few had Bibles their notebooks were crammed with the Scriptures. During the most difficult times these meetings were held at great personal risk because more than five persons gathering without permission were in danger.

When the situation became less rigid, meetings often lasted the whole day. The Christians lived in close proximity to one another so they could care for one another. The elders were the hardest working of all. They carried a heavy burden of responsibility for the flock of God. New Christians were carefully discipled. They knew well the difficulty of being a Christian in a godless society. Everyone was involved in helping others to understand God's Word and God's way — and the church in Ningchung grew.

8. A witnessing church

Deprived of their beloved pastor in 1969, the church more than ever became a witnessing church. Each member accepted the responsibility and the glad privilege of sharing the Good News. Wherever the Christians went they witnessed, despite the dangers involved in doing so. Whenever they heard of someone who was ill they were quick to offer to pray the prayer of faith and share the Good News. They witnessed by presence, by word and by deed. The multiplication of Christians thus became assured. And the church in Ningchung grew,

The "church without a pastor" is still growing. When Pastor Chung saw the way the church had grown by 1978, he felt the Lord had released him to minister elsewhere. The church in Ningchung was getting along fine. There were still many needy areas and the labourers were so few. The Lord directed him to the even more precarious ministry of an itinerant preacher.

The government completely forbids itinerant ministry because it cannot control such people. These dedicated servants of the Lord, often the most able Bible teachers, are ministering to the many house churches scattered widely over the landscape of China. They are hounded and harassed, seldom spending two nights with the same hungry saints. Often they are arrested and spend time in jail. Some are still in prison. These courageous itinerant apostles, like Pastor Chung, need our prayers. They are vital to the growth and deepening of the Church.

Pastor Chung confessed to me that when he returned in 1978 and found 5,000 believers he felt that the church in that rural area had reached its peak. But he also admitted how wrong he was — how little faith he had in the power of God and the power of the gospel. By 1987 the church of 300 had grown beyond 5,000 to over 25,000 believers scattered throughout that area. "And," said Pastor Chung, "ours is no longer the only group of Christians in the area. Besides our fellowship there are many other groups who are following the same general biblical pattern and are thus experiencing significant church growth."

TWO

THE CHURCH IN CHANG FAMILY VILLAGE

Esther Wang
A Chinese evangelist

WHEN THE JAPANESE INVADED China in 1937 their war planes rained bombs and destruction on the communities all along the coast, machine-gunning the innocent population and forcing them to flee inland to more rural areas. Among the thousands who fled was a godly lady, who left her home and property to find a more peaceful place to live.

When this lady arrived at the remote Chang Family Village, her first concern was, like Abraham, to find a place of worship. She enquired everywhere, but there was no church to be found. Sad and disappointed, she decided that she herself must start one. After saving for a time she was able to build a small church seating about 200 people, and a small house to accommodate an evangelist named Ma.

The church was located in a small market town in a flourishing farming area. The soil was rich, the farmers had good crops, and the local community prospered. After the war ended the church prospered too, and about a hundred came regularly to Sunday worship.

In 1954 at Chinese New Year time, another pastor

and I were invited to conduct special meetings. About 300 people attended, mostly coming from the surrounding region by boat or on foot. They brought their own rice and vegetables, with quilts for bedding, and camped in the large church storeroom for the duration of the meetings. There was solid evidence that the Lord was at work.

Enemy opposition

Early one morning the preacher from a church in a nearby village came to see Mr Ma, the evangelist. He was angry because many of his congregation had been attending our meetings, and he accused the evangelist of stealing his sheep. Then he came into the morning service planning to make a disturbance. I was the speaker at that service, and I hardly knew what to do. I carried on preaching and asked the Lord to prevent any interference. Praise the Lord, the Holy Spirit was at work. When I had finished speaking the visitor came to the front, knelt down to confess his sin and asked for forgiveness.

This was not the end of the Enemy's attacks. A local Communist official called a meeting for farmers which only a few attended, while many crowded into our church meetings. So he was angry and berated the people. The believers were not frightened, even in the face of this harangue. They continued to study God's Word eagerly, and prospered spiritually as well as materially.

The Enemy of souls never ceased to be active. There was much demon possession in that region, and many of the believers had themselves been delivered from demons in answer to simple, believing prayer in the Name of Jesus.

Churches closed

In 1955, during the land reform period, churches began to face increasing difficulties because of government regulations. By 1958, the year of the Great Leap Forward, some pastors were sent to prison or to labour camps because they were unwilling to obey man rather than God. Others underwent indoctrination or "brainwashing". When "people's communes" were created, almost all preachers were forced to change their profession and to work in factories. The few who compromised had no message. The church in Chang Family Village concluded that it was meaningless to keep the church open. In view of the political situation, it was best to close the doors.

Introducing Mr Yao

Among the believers in Chang Family Village was a young man by the name of Yao, whose grandmother was a very godly believer. When I visited the church in 1954 Yao was just a teenager. The Holy Spirit was at work in Mr Yao's heart and in 1961 he and another believer came to visit me in my city home, bringing a gift of vegetables. He had never been to see me before and it was unusual for a country farmer to visit the bustling city.

The Great Leap Forward had been a disaster, and famine was widespread between 1959 and 1961. The government commandeered the grain for its own use, leaving the peasants and farmers to starve. This left the people with no motivation to produce more. Realizing that Mr Yao must have suffered, I offered him ration coupons to buy food. But he declined, testifying that he knew the Lord would see him through. We had a good time of sharing and prayer together.

Years of oppression

In July 1962 I was arrested and sent to prison, where I spent the next ten years. Following that I spent another seven and a half years in a rehabilitation labour camp. I was not alone in my suffering; during the years of the Cultural Revolution all preachers came under attack. Some were paraded through the streets, some endured public trials, while others were sent to prison or faced severe persecution. Many were sentenced to long years of hard labour. Pastors and preachers would be assembled for questioning and made to accuse one another for what they had taught or said, and particularly for their critical attitude towards the government.

Under this long and intense pressure most of the pastors, one by one, denied the Lord. For a long time evangelist Ma of Chang Family Village refused to take part in accusing other pastors. But at last even he yielded to the unbearable pressure.

Pastors who refused to deny the Lord were banished to isolated places; Mr Ma was among them because the authorities were not convinced his recantation was genuine. Even though his faith did falter, he and his children continued to believe in their hearts. He would not allow his boys to attend high school lest they be sent to work far away or be pressured into joining the Communist Youth League. The family stayed together and father taught them. Members of the family later found various kinds of employment — Mr Ma himself worked as a technician in a factory, and had opportunities to witness for the Lord there.

At this time when many preachers were denying the Lord, Mr Yao also abandoned his faith and the whole family stopped reading the Bible and praying. Then Mr Yao developed cancer of the oesophagus. In desperation he and his whole family repented, confessed their sin and came back to the Lord. And the Lord had mercy on Mr Yao and healed him. After this they began to have family worship together, even though they had no Bible — all Bibles had been destroyed by the Red Guards.

Renewed contacts

Mr Yao began to enquire about me even before I was released from prison. He said that he wanted to care for me in my old age. Towards the end of 1980 he sent his younger brother to find me, and immediately invited me to lead Bible classes in Chang Family Village. Though I had been released, I was still under surveillance and anyone who came to visit me was reported. So I could not accept the invitation. Months later the invitation was repeated. I was still uncertain what to do, until one morning the verse of Scripture came to me: "Cursed is the one who is lazy to do the Lord's work," (Jer 48:10). This word kept challenging me until I was willing to obey.

In 1982, a few days before Chinese New Year, Mr Yao himself came to invite me to attend his daughter's wedding and to take part in special meetings. By this time the church had a few Bibles, and the people were hungry to learn more of the Word. One or two hours of preaching left them unsatisfied and they were prepared to listen for four or five hours at a time.

Distant outreach

Among those who attended the meetings was Brother Yao's daughter White Plum, who had brought eight new believers with her. She lived more than 100 miles away, far up in the mountains where tea was grown. Others in the district grew bamboo or had small businesses. There was also a coal mine in the valley.

White Plum was the only Christian there and the gospel was virtually unknown. She had had only two years schooling and had no special skills, but, as with the Corinthians, "God chose what is foolish in the world to shame the wise.. what is weak to shame the strong... what is low and despised..." (1 Cor 1:27, 28). White Plum was Spirit-filled and witnessed for Christ in an area where Satan had held sway for generations.

Through her faithful witness White Plum won her husband and one of her neighbours for Christ. But the neighbour's husband was strongly opposed to the gospel and began to beat her severely. He even threatened to kill her and then have White Plum pray for her to be resuscitated!

This woman went to the hospital to visit someone with whom she had quarrelled, wanting to be reconciled; there she talked about Jesus. One of the doctors ordered her not to talk about Jesus openly in the hospital, and because she was not entirely free from Satan's power, she grabbed him and hit him in the eye! This caused great confusion. The doctor reported her to the police who came to investigate, asking how and from whom she had heard about Jesus. In the end it was traced to White Plum, and people were warned to have nothing to do with her. Three jeeploads of officials arrived at White Plum's house and roughly interrogated her all day long. The Lord gave her wisdom and boldness to answer her accusers and they could find nothing to accuse her of. Fortunately, she had not been with her neighbour at the hospital that day.

The authorities took the neighbour into custody for questioning, then pronounced her "insane" and released her. After this, White Plum spent a lot of time teaching her and praying for her. Eventually the woman was delivered from demonic powers, though strange demonic activities continued in the house. Not knowing what else to do, the family invited White Plum to pray for them. As a result the demons departed, leaving the home free from their power.

Another young man in the area became possessed by demons and snapped all the iron chains with which people tried to shackle him. No one could control him. But when White Plum and the other believers prayed for him he was delivered. As a result of this deliverance and other similar miracles, many more believed in the Lord.

The number of believers continued to grow and, four years later, more than two hundred dedicated volunteers were going about preaching the gospel. Even after working long hours in the fields they would continue preaching at night. Sometimes they took time off from work to preach Christ in more distant places.

Restoring the church

During the Cultural Revolution, the church building at Chang Family Village had been used as a factory and storehouse. In 1984, when the situation began to relax, evangelist Ma sent his son to request the return of the church buildings. The authorities responded by giving an alternative plot of land and some money to build a new church. But the church now needed a larger building, and the money was insufficient. Mr Ma's family, therefore, contributed an additional RMB500[2] and other believers gave as they were able. They were determined not to borrow or go into debt.

In the summer of 1985 the Christians bought a building large enough to seat seven hundred people, and placed a large cross high on the roof where it could be seen from afar. This was important because there were no street names, so only by seeing the cross could people know where the church was located. The authorities at first ordered them to remove the cross, but Mr Ma's son explained that there had been a cross on the old church building and that churches elsewhere were allowed to display a cross. So in the end they were allowed to keep it.

Originally most of the church members had been farmers but now some owned fish farms. They would bring their fish to market each morning and were then free in the afternoon to help work on the church restoration. The deacons took responsibility for many duties such as painting and decorating.

When the work was finished, evangelist Ma and his family moved back from the countryside into the village where he was free to meet people and to talk and pray with them.

Church life

Sunday is a full day for the Christians of Chang Family Village, as in most rural churches. The peasants from all

[2] 9 RMB = £1

around start out as early as 4 am to walk to church. The service begins at 9.30 with hymn singing and prayer. Preaching begins about 10 am. Lunch is taken at noon and a second service commences at 1.30 pm. This time the speaker teaches the Scriptures and there is always an opportunity for personal testimony and sharing. Sunday is the one day in the week when Christians can get spiritual help, for most of them do not have Bibles at home.

Government regulations forbid rural churches to hold Sunday Schools and there are few meetings for young people. Only on Sundays might parents venture to bring their children to church.

The life of the peasants is very busy. All week long they work in the fields from 5 am till eight or nine in the evening, raising pigs and chickens, planting melons and so on. They also have to take their produce to market and buy the daily necessities. Water must be carried from the river, straw and fuel gathered from the mountainside and many similar tasks. To expect such busy people to take several hours to attend church meetings during the week is just not practical. Only on very special occasions can they find others to take care of the farm work, pack their bedding, prepare some food and go off to the meeting place. Christmas is a specially happy time when families with their children all come to the church to sing, recite Scripture and celebrate together.

Praying for the sick

There was a man called Fu whose mother had been paralysed and bedridden for years. He had done everything he knew to find a cure for her, but in vain. Then, when they were at their wit's end, someone urged them to repent, believe the gospel and trust in the Lord for healing. This they did and the Lord heard their prayer. The old lady was soon able to move the upper part of her body, but not her legs. Those who had led the family to the Lord exhorted them to examine their hearts further. Perhaps some unconfessed sin was hindering the complete answer to their prayers. After searching their hearts they remembered an ancestral tablet hidden in the wall. So they broke a hole in the wall, removed the tablet and burned it. Almost immediately Mrs Fu was able to move both legs.

News of this event spread and many others believed. Country folk like those in Chang Family Village are always greatly concerned when someone is ill, and believers will gather to pray for the sick one. When someone dies, all the believers in the area come to the home to express their sympathy and follow the coffin to the grave singing songs of resurrection. Unbelievers witnessing a Christian funeral often become interested and begin to attend the house meetings or the church to hear the gospel.

Training a new generation

The church at Chang Family Village continued to grow and urgently needed more leaders. In May 1983 I was invited to hold ten days of training classes for Christian workers.

The classes began the day I arrived. Early the next morning, about 4 am, someone knocked on my door while I was praying and urged me to leave quickly. The authorities had gone to Mr Yao's home in a nearby village and confiscated all the books he had received from abroad. Two young believers had been arrested and taken off to prison. For my own safety the brother was urging me to leave.

Should I go or stay? I suggested that he should ask the pastor's advice. After prayer and fasting we decided that I should stay on to conduct the training classes. Nothing untoward happened, and the Lord was with us as we studied the Scriptures daily throughout the full ten days.

These training classes were held at all seasons of the year. In winter, students gladly put up with extremely spartan conditions — sleeping on the floor and eating the most frugal of meals. Well-to-do businessmen sacrificed time to join the classes. In the summer vacation season, grade school teachers joined the evangelistic teams and even undertook to do the cooking so that the ladies could study in the Bible classes.

During 1985 and 1986, opportunities to hold Bible training classes in the village increased. Many new believers had changed their lifestyle and were anxious to serve the Lord. Among these was a brother named Yang.

Once, while waiting for a bus, Mr Yang witnessed to a couple he met by the roadside and told them about the love of God, the death of Jesus on the Cross and His resurrection. They had never before heard the gospel. The next time he was passing that way he met the same couple again, and asked them if they had yet believed. "Yes, we believe," they replied.

The man had always been a heavy smoker, but now he had given up the habit completely. Their son was in Middle School, a rare thing for a country boy. This young man was a member of the Communist Youth

League in school and strongly opposed his parents becoming Christians. He even made threats against them. Then one day when he came home from school, he saw unused tobacco in his father's room, tobacco which he had bought for his father at a time when it was difficult to buy. When he asked his father about it and found that he had given up smoking, he was deeply affected. "What power there is in believing!" he exclaimed.

Because of this the son also believed. At first he went to hear the gospel secretly and prayed in secret. But when fellow students discovered what he was doing they reported him to the principal, who called an accusation meeting and forced the boy to undergo self-criticism. This was repeated several times. In the end, the principal told him he must either leave the Lord or leave the school. The boy chose to leave the school and to follow the Lord and preach the gospel.

Another person who attended the classes was a great gambler. His father, a Communist Party member, constantly kept an eye on his son to keep him from gambling, but without success. Once he went up a mountain to gamble in secret with his friends, but he lost all his money. His mother gave him RMB60 to buy clothes, but instead he spent it all on gambling. Then he borrowed RMB20 from his sister, again to "buy clothes", and told his mother they cost RMB60. He said they were good quality and his mother believed him.

God intervened in this young man's life. He heard the gospel, repented and stopped gambling. His father had previously regarded all Christians as scum, but his attitude changed and he began to respect this son who now loved Jesus and spent all his spare time studying the Bible and leading others to Christ.

The growth of these rural churches has been due to the fact that believers go everywhere preaching the gospel. They often travel by night on foot, by bicycle (except in the mountains) or by bus (although the buses are always crowded). Tobacco smokers, gamblers and devotees of the occult are among those who have come to Christ through the church in Chang Family Village. Even Communists have observed the change that Christ makes in a life and have themselves been won to Christ.

The power of God is being mightily demonstrated through the gospel in China today. What a wonderful Saviour we have! What a mighty God is ours! May all the glory be to Him, King of kings and Lord of lords!

THREE

WHERE A CELESTIAL EMPIRE BEGAN

A former missionary

.ONE HUNDRED YEARS AGO massive floods caused widespread famine in some coastal provinces of North China. Thousands of families migrated west in search of food, trekking more than eight hundred miles. They eventually arrived in an area depopulated by the Taiping Rebellion and later by repeated Muslim invasions.

Among these migrants was a group of ten Christian families who, in 1891, settled on a plot of land and built a village to which they gave a gospel name. The life of this small Christian community was based on the New Testament. They set aside a small hut for Sunday worship, and a year later, forty Christians formed themselves into the first Protestant church in that part of China. Soon they attempted to evangelize their neighbours, but feeling their need of assistance, especially in education and in medical care, they sent a request for help to British missionaries in the neighbouring province.

In response to this call, two men arrived in the area. They wrote home to England, "We hope that these Christians may become the leaven in the larger mass of their migrating fellow-countrymen." Thus the church began to grow in the surrounding villages, several of which also adopted Christian names. There was some opposition, but nothing to compare with that offered by the local city inhabitants. With their fierce provincial pride in a great imperial past, they hated all outsiders and regarded Christians and Christian culture as foreign and therefore to be resisted. So the gates of the provincial capital were firmly closed to missionaries.

Initial growth

At first, therefore, church growth was confined to the immigrant rural community. But when a Christian doctor arrived to open a hospital in the city, attitudes changed. Grateful patients who had found Christ in the hospital spread the Good News among their families and friends in the villages. Progress in the city, however, was frequently interrupted by famines and long sieges by war-lords. Twice missionaries had to be evacuated. After the first Communist uprising in 1925 and the start of the civil war, the church was twice attacked by anti-foreign mobs. The anti-foreign movement forced missions to speed up the policy of indigenisation.

As other missionary societies began to arrive in the city, a growing comity between missionaries and newly-independent churches led to the formation of a United Church Council in 1925. Its objective was for the church speedily to attain self-support, self-government and self-propagation. Thus the Holy Spirit used political events to help lay a firm foundation for the church in this remote region, so that not even the power of a totalitarian and atheistic regime would prevail against it. It was a church which, even when driven underground, continued to grow.

The war with Japan not only created even more opportunities for church growth, but also brought an influx of gifted Christians who were fugitives from the Japanese invaders. Among them came the messengers of revival who brought great blessing to the church. Extremes were avoided by an annual two weeks Bible school, where the Christians learned to understand the Corinthian experience and its meaning for the church.

In the city, missionaries were presented with many opportunities for outreach: for example, a radio station which allowed gospel broadcasts and an opening into schools and factories. Summer schools for college students resulted in many decisions for Christ, and a new bookroom operated a system of circulating libraries.

Yet formidable hindrances to growth remained. The insularity of the local people, their materialistic lifestyle, and moral weakness among some church leaders all contributed to the spiritual deadness of the city church. The narrow, parochial outlook of the city Christians led to the formation of cliques. Because the church was mainly anti-intellectual, the Christians regarded students and other intelligent young people as dangerous. Even the teachers and students in the church school were not closely involved with the church.

Eventually, through a weekly meeting for prayer and mutual encouragement, God breathed new life into the dry bones. Keen young people began to come into the church and helped to build it up with new Christians and new leaders. At last the city church began to grow, and new churches were planted in the suburbs. God brought together a people of love and power at just the right time so they were prepared for 1949, the year when, in Mao's words, the people of China "stood up".

Cold winds blow

In 1950 the new government began to tie strings of political indoctrination and propaganda around the church and, although the 13 pastors continued working as before, church growth was outwardly checked. Direction of labour and a six-day working week kept everybody extremely busy, while Sunday was the day for political rallies, sports and indoctrination lectures. Such was the pressure on the minds of school children that they were afraid to go to church or Sunday school, and would even opt out of family prayers. Eventually the government imposed a new church constitution and, by February 1951, all mission property had been handed over and all foreign personnel withdrawn from China. The era of foreign missions had ended.

God had overruled the apparently haphazard beginnings to create the lasting miracle of a truly indigenous church, free from the denominational debris and divisions deposited in China by the western church.

God in the silence

A Chinese muleteer once said to a missionary, "Do you see that tree, pastor?" He pointed to a solitary pine beside a grave mound on the summit of a lofty hill, and asked, "How do you think it grew up there?" Nobody had thought about this. His answer was: "A man scrambled up there with two buckets of water every day for several weeks until the young sapling got a start. Now it grows by itself! This," he went on, "is a parable of the church which, watered by the emotions, the prayers and the labours of missionaries prior to 1951, did not die when the cold winds of persecution blew, but continued to grow."

After 1951, news reached the outside world in scanty gleanings from travellers. The educational institutions and hospitals were taken over by the Communist authorities and secularized. All approaches to young people were halted. The incessant anti-imperialist and anti-religious propaganda was more intense in this remote region than elsewhere. Witness for Christ became increasingly difficult and dangerous, while pastors were required to engage in manual labour seven days a week.

Despite it all, news came in 1956 that, in the past two years, four new churches had been built and others repaired, and that 350 people had been baptized. In the countryside, 13 main churches and 89 branch churches were still functioning with a total membership of about 3,000. In 1959, just after the Great Leap Forward, a traveller reported that Christians were still meeting together in the city. But then came 1966!

The Cultural Revolution

As the "Great Proletarian Cultural Revolution" burst on the nation, what had been intimidation became extermination. Along with Christians across the nation, the believers in this area struggled to survive. Without access to any church building and without Bibles, hymnbooks or other Christian materials, a remnant of about 30 people continued to meet regularly in a former Christian bookseller's home to pray and praise in Christian worship. It was he who held together the people of God in the "bonds of love" and in "the fellowship of Christ's sufferings".

A new day

In 1980, the exciting news reached the West that churches in Shanghai and other eastern cities of China had been reopened. Around that time a letter from the bookseller conveyed the welcome news that the bamboo curtain had lifted also in his city, that the main church had been reopened and that it was possible once more for a person openly to declare himself a Christian.

The letter described the opening service when believers flocked in from all parts of the city and from the villages. The church was packed, with many standing outside in the courtyard. The preacher was one of the elderly pastors of 30 years ago. He preached the gospel, the Holy Spirit worked mightily and every believer was inspired to follow Jesus. One of the city churches had been demolished, but extensive repairs were carried out on other church buildings.

An American tourist reported the phenomenal growth of the 20 to 30 house churches in and around the city. The one which he attended met every Sunday with a congregation of about 200, and held a Bible study group on Thursdays to study the book of Romans. Bibles were in short supply and the only other books available were *Pilgrim's Progress*, *Streams in the Desert* and a biography of Hudson Taylor.

Another visitor reported on the celebration of Christmas in the main church where the congregation numbered 600 to 700. The bookseller also wrote describing the Christmas services, and expressing gratitude for Bibles. He told how God had graciously been answering the prayers of overseas friends. Christmas that year had been much better than in the past! Four congregations had met in one church to sing God's praises and large numbers of people had attended. More than 250 also met in his own home. In other places there were 300 to 500. He added: "More than thirty years ago you planted seeds, and now the time has come to gather the harvest! The believers really stand firm for Jesus and worship God in reality. We believe God is guiding the church He forged in the fire. Please keep on praying. (Signed) Your little brother in Jesus Christ."

The church continued to grow. In 1981, despite fierce persecution, 50 churches were operating in the city with scores of house churches among the original settlers in the countryside. In 1982, two of these churches were each holding three services on Sunday with overflowing congregations, as well as a weekly Bible study service. One pastor told visiting missionary friends of 7,000 recent conversions.

In one small town where missionaries had planted the church in 1913, it had grown to only 150 believers by 1951. Yet between 1978 and 1980 over 2,700 people were baptized there, 500 of them worshipping in the original church building. Altogether in that area 20 "meeting points" with a total attendance of 5,000 had been established. The one and only pastor desperately needed co-workers to help shepherd the flock.

Fresh opposition

In 1983, all communication with this growing church ceased and silence fell again. One reason was that the former bookroom manager and chief letter-writer had been killed in an accident. But the main problem was the government drive against "superstitious practices".

The Religious Affairs Bureau began to clamp down on all unofficial religious groups. Some house church leaders were imprisoned for two years and the church was subjected to investigation and discrimination.

In 1985 Christian travellers reported that the two main city churches were served by eight ministers and 14 elders originally from different denominations. They were cooperating with other large neighbouring churches in the running of Short Term Bible Seminars which attracted 60 students. The total number of registered Christians in this city and its suburbs was reckoned to be about 16,000 in 1987, with more in the unregistered house churches and at least another 1,000 fellowships in the countryside. And they still proliferate! Praise be to God who leads the Christian Church forward on her long march, making the wrath of man to praise Him!

The character of the worship

In the city churches the character of the worship has changed very little since 1951. The remarkable enthusiasm and spiritual vitality of the Body of Christ elsewhere is not exhibited there, certainly not in the ways we associate with many growing and renewed churches in the West. Nevertheless, though the routine is the same as before, there is true joy and a warmth of fellowship. A choir leads the singing. Prayer is offered and a Bible portion relating to the subject of the sermon is read by different leaders. Then follows a long and discursive, if not dull, sermon, devoid of histrionics or emotional appeal. And yet, as one observer reported, the whole service communicated what could only be described as a strong sense of hope.

How then can we explain the packed congregations and the massive increase in membership? There is no glory or glamour in the services of these city churches to attract people. And yet, as the pastor said goodbye to a visitor at the door and the crowds were dispersing, he remarked, "We no longer need to go out to them: now they come to us!"

The aching void

The Revolution has met the basic physical needs of the people. They now have the promised "bowl of rice". But the very materialistic nature of government policies has left an aching void, a hunger in the hearts of the people. Today, Jesus, through His disciples, is supplying the multitudes with the living bread, His saving love, as literally and as simply as He did in Palestine. The traditional gregariousness of the Chinese finds its counterpart in the loving, sharing "togetherness" of the family of God, the openness and the intimacy of being "in Christ". This, too, is attracting the common people to Christ as it did in New Testament times.

"A church persecuted is a church purified" and therefore a church powerful. Masses are being attracted to a fellowship of people who have been refined in the furnace of affliction, are certain about what they believe and whose sole allegiance is to the Living Christ. This church has out-sacrificed an atheistic dictatorship with all its draconian demands. Even when, in the frightening "accusation meetings", Christians were expected to denounce other members of the Christian family, they flaunted their faith, proudly displaying a cross and being counted for Christ.

One pastor in this city church was imprisoned, his

only crime being that he followed Christ. When he was near to death because of his sufferings, his fellow prisoners persuaded him to eat because, they said, he must survive or his congregation would have no one to lead them in future. Today, in his eighties, he is back, white-haired and almost transparent, a living witness to the power of Christ. He and others like him say they knew that Christians overseas were praying for them; they, too, were praying for the churches overseas.

This church is growing as never before. "Once we had to go out to preach the gospel," the leaders say, "now people are coming to us to discuss the Christian faith and all our leaders are kept very busy meeting the demands."

This explains why one city church needs so many pastors. It is, of course, a post-denominational church with the pastors representing different denominations. But even with so many pastors the ratio of pastors to members is still only 1 to 500. Most of the pastors are elderly, while the famine of the Word of God has created a great hunger of the spirit yearning to be satisfied. Also, government demands for full statistical details of baptisms, baptismal candidates and all church activities require an enormous amount of administration and form-filling.

House churches[3]

This church maintains a close relationship with the house churches in the area. It meets with them and seeks to serve them both in preaching and in presiding over Communion services. About 10,000 such groups

[3] See page 11

are connected with this church. "Official or unofficial", one pastor said, "we cooperate, all working together for the Kingdom of God." This attitude is very courageous as well as Christian because, as late as 1987, a house church evangelist in a northern area was fined RMB2,500 after detention for three months. Other house church leaders have been arrested and have spent terms in prison.

The outlook

In a land where the government rejects any belief in the concept of God, none dare to predict the future. But, since China is and always will be under the sovereignty of God, we should be filled with hope. The church of this survey certainly is a growing church. The Long March which began in the 1880s cannot be halted. Arnold Toynbee's words "... a single figure rises from the flood and straightway fills the whole horizon" point to the Saviour, of whom it is written "the will of the Lord shall prosper in His hand; He shall see the fruit of the travail of His soul and be satisfied."

FOUR

GOD AT WORK IN VANITY FAIR

Valiant for Truth, a Christian professional

UNDER DENG XIAOPING the Communist Party adopted more moderate and open policies and encouraged the tourist trade. More and more areas of China were being opened to foreign visitors. So in 1982 we returned[4] for the first time, planning to visit Christian churches in nine great cities of China. Conditions had greatly improved, the churches were alive and well after years of persecution, martyrdom and suffering, and the Christians were free to worship in newly reopened and refurbished churches.

An unforgettable train journey

We travelled by express train to the city of Vanity Fair, and even on the journey saw evidences of active evangelism. We were sharing a four-berth compartment with Mr Ma, a government cadre in the city's planning department, and Mr Tam, a young machinery salesman and a Buddhist. As the sun rose, we were crossing one of China's beautiful rivers. Mr Ma burst into joyful song and suggested that I should write

[4] Valiant for Truth and his wife Loving Virtue spent some years in China before 1949, and then lived in Hong Kong for a time.

about this in my diary.

Later, two young men and a girl invited themselves into the compartment and embarked on a vigorous discussion about Christianity and Christians with Communist Mr Ma and Buddhist Mr Tam. I had already noticed the girl seated in the corridor reading her New Testament and Psalms, and singing Psalm 23 quietly to herself to a lovely, new, irregular Chinese melody. The three freely reported that they were returning from the north, where they had held a week's evangelistic meetings in a large open space in the hills. Nightly attendance was 150 to 200 people. Some of these had become Christians, including one married couple.

Suddenly, the public address system appealed for any doctor on the train to attend a sick man in another coach. My wife, accompanied by a young Chinese named Francis, went to offer help. They had the man taken to hospital at the next station. On their return to their seats Francis, a worker in a watch factory and a lapsed Roman Catholic, joined us in the compartment. We told him the story of Paley the scientist using a watch for an illustration and concluding that the universe, like a watch, must have a Designer and Maker. Francis listened thoughtfully.

The evangelists did not seem to mind that Mr Ma was a Communist cadre, but continued their long discussion with him and Mr Tam about Communism, Buddhism and Christianity. Later Mr Ma, left alone with me, talked most affectionately and expressed sorrow that we might never meet again. In his hometown, he said, Communists and Christians were cooperating in building a new society. This, he felt, was a good thing.

We had a moving farewell as he left the train.

The church in Vanity Fair

Vanity Fair is a large city where Christians are both numerous and faithful. A thousand worshippers flocked to Sunday services at one of the churches, which had a robed choir of forty singers. The service was led by a team of five ministers. The church leaders told us that 3,000 had attended both the Christmas and Easter celebrations. At a second church, 800 attended each Sunday, while 1,000 people overflowed the Christmas service. Their youth group was 400 strong, of whom 50 had attended a Christian youth conference earlier in the year. In the Catholic church (use of the word "Roman" is not permitted by the Religious Affairs Bureau) 400 regularly attend Mass and many of their young people had also attended a youth conference that year. The priest told us how, during the Cultural Revolution, a large fire had been started in the nave, fuelled by wooden pews and church books. Young artists were now painting new "stations of the Cross".

In each church, Loving Virtue and I were welcomed with interest. At one Sunday service, my wife found herself sitting next to a young woman doctor of traditional medicine whose parents were Christians. She herself had also discovered that, in a Marxist society, the only answer to life's problems was faith in Jesus Christ, so she had decided to believe and to follow Him. Another time I found myself sitting near an American visitor accompanied by some American Chinese. He said he was an attorney in President Reagan's office and prayed daily for the President and for the Secretary of the Communist Party, Mr Hu Yaobang.

Pitfalls

In another city, a day's journey from Vanity Fair, we met Christian friends from earlier days. One has since been ordained and is the pastor of the local church. Another was a senior master in the Middle School. Through him the headmaster invited us to address their one thousand pupils. We were asked to teach English lessons in individual classes and to give a lecture in English to two hundred teachers from other schools. In the privacy of the teachers' common room we were able to share some of our life's experiences and convictions with each other. All had suffered in the Cultural Revolution, besides losing ten years of education. They described that time as the "ten terrible years". Sadly, our teacher friend later faced a public "accusation meeting" and was made to confess his error in inviting two foreign missionaries to the school.

Invitation to teach in Vanity Fair

Three years later, in 1985, Loving Virtue and I returned to teach English at the university in Vanity Fair. The sense of freedom seemed even greater than before. Reconstruction fever was everywhere apparent and the university campus resembled a building site. This energy was reflected in the churches, in the thronging city and among the large number of university students.

As salaried teachers on contract, we felt obliged simply to teach English and to avoid sharing our religious faith openly. Instead, we asked the Holy Spirit to lead enquirers to us and to give us opportunities to speak a word of witness during lectures, since both the Bible and Christianity were recognized as elements of English culture. Our opportunities were sometimes startling.

However, we constantly remembered a common Chinese proverb: "Bend your head when the eaves are low!"

Our university commitments only allowed us to visit churches on Sundays. At one church we noticed that other foreign teachers who attended were officially welcome, but only as visitors sharing the times of worship. The congregation consisted largely of older people. Bibles printed in Shanghai were readily available, but in the old script. Some university students openly attended this church and two of them were preparing for baptism.

Picnics and an Easter celebration

Students in our own class regularly invited us to join them in picnics to various memorial parks or famous buildings dedicated to their Chinese heroes. We soon found ourselves visiting a park commemorating some of the early martyrs of the People's Revolution. Shortly after this visit a student deputation came to see us.

"We hope you enjoyed your visit to the park," said their spokesman. "And since your Easter festival is near, can you tell us how to observe it?"

Taken by surprise, we simply said: "Well, naturally we go to church."

"May we all come with you?" they asked cheerfully.

We hesitated before suggesting: "That might not be wise. To take 50 of you to the local church would attract a lot of attention, and lead to questions and maybe criticism of ourselves and you and the local church from your university officials."

Wiser heads in the group agreed. "Yes, indeed! So could you give us instead an extra lecture on Easter?"

"If you ask the opinion and obtain the permission of your professor, we would certainly be glad to do that," we replied.

The professor heartily agreed to the suggestion and a two-hour extra lecture was arranged for the following Saturday — normally a free day. In preparation for the lecture Loving Virtue bought 50 steamed dumplings as a substitute for hot cross buns, and 50 fresh eggs which she boiled and decorated with Easter symbols whose significance she would explain. I prepared broadsheets of information about Jesus, giving historic details of His birth, life, crucifixion and resurrection in the context of Jewish history and culture, with two maps in English and two hymns in both languages.

Loving Virtue told the Easter story most vividly, while I added appropriate headings on the blackboard. The students showed great interest, enjoying the dumplings and taking the eggs and broadsheets home to their families in some excitement. The lecture was followed by a celebration at a famous restaurant with ourselves as guests. Chinese students love any excuse for an outing and a meal.

In the course of my teaching I had asked students to write English diaries, returning them for marking each week. The diaries following the lecture contained most interesting comments. Some said they had never heard the Easter story before. Others wrote that their parents were or had once been Christians. Some even confessed that they themselves were believers. But it would have been very brave for any students to show open personal commitment. This could attract disciplinary reaction from the Party. We realized afresh that the Holy Spirit is not restricted to organized church activity. "The wind blows wherever it pleases" as the following story shows.

An Easter church service

A student friend told us about a Mandarin-speaking church further away. Being Mandarin speakers ourselves, we gratefully accepted his offer to take us there. We found a large congregation present and were warmly welcomed, sensing a feeling of deep joy in the people and the worship. On Easter Day we set off early, in showers and stormy winds, to return to this church. It was beautifully decorated with flowers and brilliantly lit by candelabra. The place was full to overflowing with both young and old. We managed to squeeze in next to an African student friend from the university. A small children's choir, dressed in colourful capes, led in a large adult robed choir of 30 or so. The children sang two joyous Easter action songs. Then the whole congregation rose to sing with exultant joy the familiar "Jesus Christ is risen today", complete with Hallelujahs. The Scripture was well read and the prayers were strong and moving. The Easter hymns produced a great volume of praise and the adult choir sang two lovely anthems. A sudden, fierce thunderstorm, with brilliant lightning and torrential rain joined in the praises! The window shutters were quickly closed and everyone sang even more joyously.

The sermon was the most dynamic Easter message we had ever heard. An older minister preached in Mandarin in short, vigorous sentences. A younger man interpreted in the equally emphatic local dialect. The atmosphere was electric, excited, joyous. Every few minutes, the preachers would cry out:

"So you must believe and open your hearts to the

risen Lord Jesus!" or

"We must repent and believe, for Jesus is alive. Give yourselves to Him!"

The double impact of Mandarin and the local dialect was unbelievably compelling. Any moment I thought the whole congregation, including myself, would be moved to cry out "Hallelujah! Hallelujah!" and clap their hands. The double sermon lasted one hour and seemed only half that time.

As the final hymn rang out with heartfelt fervour, children came in carrying paper bags of hard-boiled Easter eggs. Some greeted the visitors by shaking hands, saying "Happy Easter!" One gently rubbed the hands of our African neighbour as if uncertain whether the colour came off! Many adults greeted us quietly with deep pleasure, saying "Jesus is risen!" The official ushers said, "Please come again."

Unexpected witness

Another time, my students at the university were studying an American text book. The day's lesson was a newspaper article about Bob Dylan, the famous American folk singer, describing his involvement with drugs and alcoholism and his sudden disappearance from the US teenage scene. The article revealed how Dylan had unexpectedly reappeared, telling the media that he had been converted to Christ and was "born again" and freed from his former addictions.

"Born again" being a Bible phrase, I asked the students to comment on its meaning. After some hesitation and several confused suggestions, one student replied: "It is to become a new person by being changed completely from the inside to the outside of our being!"

No further comment from me seemed necessary.

Illness strikes

Loving Virtue was suddenly struck down with a severe virus illness which left her prostrate. She was taken to hospital where the medical staff gradually nursed her back to health, used both western and traditional Chinese medicine and showed very loving care.

During her convalescence, almost all her students began to visit her. Being in a private room (with only an occasional fellow patient) she had many opportunities to talk with her visitors, who felt free to discuss her Christian faith openly and to ask about the Bible. On her bedside table were copies of the New Testament and the Gospels, which visitors would pick up and read. One hospital orderly who brought her meals would just sit there reading through a Gospel. Some began to realize that the Bible was not merely a great literary treasure and to ask for copies. Gradually we gave away every copy we had. One Marxist student asked for a New Testament and, a few days later, rushed after me on the campus saying: "I have almost finished that New Testament. Can you get me a complete Bible?"

Another Christian student whom we called Paul, who was preparing for baptism, came by night like Nicodemus to talk about his spiritual struggles. I urged him: "Do not trust your own feelings or let your fears overwhelm you. Simply trust Jesus as Lord. His Holy Spirit will do in you what you cannot do of yourself. And use a modern Chinese Bible to help you understand the Lord's teaching." He listened quietly, then said, "Will you please give me your own testimony of the Lord's reality and His dealings with you?"

As we were talking, an older student called in and asked if he could visit Loving Virtue. So all three of us went to the hospital together. On the way, the two students began talking together and Paul testified to the other about his Christian faith. Having seen my wife, the older student returned home, while Paul asked Loving Virtue to share her testimony. Then he asked both of us to pray for him as Satan was attacking and undermining his faith. After we had prayed, he too prayed aloud himself, most earnestly and movingly. Spiritual and anti-spiritual forces are very real to these young Chinese Christians. This was equally true in apostolic times.

Farewell to Vanity Fair

While my wife was seriously ill, I had to look after myself. I had also taken on extra lectures as well as visiting the hospital two or three times a day. One morning I awoke feeling that I had come to the end of my strength. I read 2 Corinthians 6 with new insight. The Apostle's inner strength seemed to accuse me.

With the increasing summer heat, now 96 degrees fahrenheit and the humidity 98%, my energy seeped away. Age wearied me. Pride beset me. Faith in God's grace challenged me. China called me to stay. Home beckoned us to go. The decision must soon be made. Surely the Lord would provide replacements for us if we left. And He did! Six foreign Christian teachers became available. We could return home and the witness would be maintained.

Eventually, my wife was well enough to leave hospital. She paid a last visit to her students who urged her to give a final lecture. With no lesson material to hand, she borrowed an English magazine from a student. That morning her Bible meditation had been "God is light" and the magazine contained an article on "Light". With her gentle smile, she gave a simple scientific explanation of light, finally adding: "Of course, I am a Christian and I believe that the light of the universe is the creation of God Himself!"

The students laughed and applauded out of their joy and love for their teacher, despite the underlying regret at our departure. Truly, the Holy Spirit's activity is not restricted to the routine of Sunday worship or the organized church.

FIVE

CHINA'S JERUSALEM

A former pastor's son

THE CHURCH OF WENZHOU *(Zhejiang Province) traces its origin to the 1870s. One of the first party of missionaries to sail for China with Hudson Taylor under the banner of the China Inland Mission had only one leg! But it was he who began proclaiming the gospel in Wenzhou. Hudson Taylor himself baptized the first converts. Early missionary activities included schools and a hospital. In the 1930s, due to anti-western agitation and student strikes, the schools were all closed down. As the church grew, regular local Bible schools ensured a church with strong roots, grounded in the Word of God. Evangelism was always a priority and the Chinese pastor sometimes accompanied the missionaries into bandit-infested areas to preach the gospel.*

During the thirties, Watchman Nee in Shanghai began training leaders for the expansion of the assemblies. The major expansion took place in the coastal provinces of Fujian and Zhejiang. By 1940, in Zhejiang alone, the "Little Flock", as these indigenous assemblies were nicknamed, numbered 262 with a total membership of 39,000. Solid Bible teaching by Chinese teachers not only ensured the survival of the Little Flock assemblies in the years of persecution, but also laid the foundation for the spectacular numerical growth of all the churches in both coastal provinces from the late 1970s onward.

In 1951, when the missionaries withdrew from China, there were four or five large and flourishing churches in Wenzhou and hundreds of country congregations with a total of over 5,000 believers in this one city and the surrounding areas alone. Many of the merchants were Christians and ten shops in one street declared themselves closed on Sundays. The Christian influence on the city economy was considerable and Wenzhou is now one of the wealthiest cities in China. The CIM church was undoubtedly the largest and strongest ever to be planted by the China Inland Mission.

This story is written by the pastor's son, who is now living in the USA.

One family's experiences

As the Communists imposed their regime on the Chinese people after 1949, the suffering of Christians began almost immediately in a subtle but real way.

During the Cultural Revolution, one large family of Christians in this city was a prime target of persecution, because they were such shining witnesses for Christ. First, the Red Guards ransacked their home, carrying away Bibles and other religious books, together with valuable items. Then they took the grandmother into custody, and later humilated her by parading her through the streets with her two hands tied together behind her, a dunce's hat on her head and a board hanging around her neck stating her "crime". Her elderly husband, a leader of the local congregation, was left sick and bedridden at home. The beating of gongs attracted spectators, and the old lady was ordered to stand at the entrance of the primary school her grandchildren were attending, to be publicly "struggled" against. The grandchildren were too ashamed to look at her. Not long after this the sick grandfather passed away. God spared him from public humiliation and abuse.

Because of their family connection, the grandchildren were abused, ridiculed and treated as subhuman. They dared not enter or leave the school by the main entrance or play with the other students during recess for fear of their militant schoolmates. They had become outcasts of society.

This elderly couple's oldest son was arrested for involvement in evangelism. He was a true man of God and also a respected and learned member of society. He subsequently died as a martyr in a Communist prison cell, leaving behind four children from ten years old to a few months. They have all grown up to be mature Christians.

The next blow fell when the elderly couple's daughter, the mother of young children, was arrested and publicly abused. She, too, was paraded through the streets, attracting big crowds of spectators. Her young children felt pain and shame at seeing their mother led through the streets with her head shaven and a board with a cross on it hanging around her neck.

It is traditional in China, at the New Year festival, to paste red posters with positive words on the doorposts at the entrance to every house. In the case of mourning in a family, white posters are used instead. The Red Guards spitefully pasted white posters on the doorpost of this family's home in order to shame them. The police often checked the house at night in search of strangers, since the family were accustomed to show hospitality to fellow Christians and other travellers.

The children used to hide from other children so as to avoid their contempt. When they took food to their mother in prison, they did so stealthily to avoid being seen. Not surprisingly, the children became rather introvert.

Good jobs and opportunities in higher education were usually denied to children of Christian families. However one of the children of this family was an exception. Due to God's amazing grace and through several miraculous turns of events this young man, named Aimian, not only finished college in China but was able to study for a PhD in a large university in the United States. He is a strong Christian and is effectively witnessing among other students from mainland China. He is willing to serve God wherever He leads, whether that means returning to China or staying in North America.

Going underground

In spite of much persecution, Christians in this city did not turn back. Instead, they went on showing zeal for the Lord and for lost souls, and some continued to spread the gospel far and wide. But there was a price to be paid. Some were jailed and others executed. Many escaped arrest because Christians working in the police offices would give advance warning of searches.

Christian gatherings never ceased completely even during the Cultural Revolution. When political pressure ran high, churches went underground. As soon as the pressures relaxed, gatherings immediately resumed.

Once, the police arrested a group of Christians gathered for prayer in a Christian woman's home. They left the woman herself free to take care of her household. However, as soon as she could find a friend to take her place, she hastened to join the arrested group. Such behaviour bewildered the authorities, but she explained, "We Christians who suffer for the Lord on earth will receive a crown in heaven. I don't want to miss that!"

The group of twelve were, as usual, paraded through the streets, but they had peace and joy in their hearts as their actions testified to the power and glory of the gospel of Jesus Christ.

Costly faithfulness

The body life of Christians was maintained even during the darkest hours. One local preacher named Chow was condemned to labour camp in a remote region of the country. He left behind a pregnant wife and several children. Instead of feeling sorry for himself, he was able to minister comfort to others in similar circumstances. In spite of hostile threats and against friendly advice, he continued to preach Christ, running the risk of being even more severely punished.

The Christians in Wenzhou took good care of his family and, when he returned after more than fifteen years of exile, he found his children grown into adulthood and the family in excellent condition. Mr Chow is now over seventy and is still active in Christian service.

Demotion

One local Christian named Chen, an accountant and also a leader in the church, had a deep love for lost souls and was brave enough to lead others in his work unit to the Lord. He shared the gospel with a leader in the Red Guards, a man who had a vicious character. At first, when invited to Christian homes to hear the gospel, this man used to carry a gun with him. But after he had accepted the Lord his life was completely changed. He turned in his gun and resigned from the Red Guard organization.

Not surprisingly, this action infuriated his superiors, who staged a big public meeting to "struggle" both with him and Mr Chen. They demanded that they either renounce their faith publicly or be demoted to sanitary workers.

There was no sewer system in those rural areas and to be a sanitary worker was a filthy and disgusting occupation. It involved getting up at midnight to collect human excrement from each house and then carry the heavy load by carrying pole to designated locations. These workers also had to endure the bitter cold of winter nights.

Refusing to deny the Lord, both men publicly accepted the demotion. Mr Chen's family was very concerned about his health as he had seldom done hard labour and had already undergone major surgery. But the family committed his life into the hands of the Lord who promised: "Never will I leave you; never will I forsake you." He continued as a sanitary worker for more than twelve years until his retirement, without ever falling ill.

A large house church

In retrospect, Mr Chen was glad that he had obeyed God's will in a time of crisis. The local financial system was in a mess because the Red Guards were using money from public funds for extravagant personal spending. As an accountant, Mr Chen would either have had to collaborate with the Red Guards or offend them. His demotion was God's way of taking him out of that situation, so that he might have a clear conscience to serve the Lord later as a lay minister of a local congregation.

Now, in Wenzhou, there is a new congregation of several hundred believers with their own new building. This is one of the largest house churches in China today. The many thousands of Christians in the district meet in hundreds of meeting points. It has become almost impossible for the security police to enforce government restrictions on religious activities.

A faithful teacher

One young man from a Christian family was teaching at a college in a neighbouring city. He had experienced God's love and mercy in his life but, as a teacher, he was forbidden to support any religion or participate in religious activities. The penalty for violating this regulation was dismissal from his teaching post. Students breaking it would be dismissed or assigned to undesirable jobs on graduation.

However, this young Christian was not intimidated by such threats. He took the initiative to gather Christian students and faculty members together to share and encourage one another. Most of them were far from home and reluctant to attend the government-supported churches, so they felt the need for mutual encouragement to keep their faith strong. God blessed their fellowship, their numbers increased and they enjoyed peace without outside interference. This Christian young man wrote, "What was not allowed by man was allowed by God."

God our refuge

During those dark nights of oppression, many Christians personally experienced the truth of Psalm 46,

> "God is our refuge and strength, an ever present help in trouble. Therefore we will not fear, though the earth give way and the mountains fall into the heart of the sea, though its waters roar and foam and the mountains quake with their surging."

Some schoolmates of Christian students were killed in battles between different units of the Red Guards. But in Wenzhou no God-fearing young people participated in the Red Guards' activities. They found safety at home with their families. At this time conflicts occurred not only on the streets between strangers, but also between husband and wife, father and son, brothers and sisters. In contrast, Christians enjoyed love and care, not only within their own families but also with other Christian families.

Prayer prevails

In 1966 the churches of Wenzhou, in common with all the churches of China, were closed down by the Red Guards. The church leaders called for three months of prayer and fasting. Small meetings resumed in 1967, only to provoke intensified opposition and fierce persecution.

In about 1978, a powerful work of the Holy Spirit began, bringing thousands of men and women, and especially young people, to Christ. The growth was prolific, and renewed persecution failed to quench the fires of revival. Even children remained true to the Lord despite threats from their teachers. In some communes the majority of the members became Christians and one commune of 10,000 people was 100% Christian. The commune officials named the production teams "Jesus team No. 1, Jesus team No. 2", and recommended other communes to "emulate the Jesus teams" which consistently reached high production levels!

This phenomenal growth has continued. According to some estimates, as high as 20% of the population of Wenzhou are Christians. It has been called the "Jerusalem" or "Holy Land" of China. There are 320,000 Christians in the Wenzhou area and, according to the China News Agency, 4,000 Party members have joined the ranks of believers.

Secrets of growth

What is the secret of this phenomenal church growth? It seems to lie in the willingness of Christians to suffer for Christ. That has been the armour which has overcome the adversary. In I Peter 4 we read, "Therefore, since Christ suffered in His body, arm yourselves also with the same attitude, because he who has suffered in his body is done with sin." Adopting this attitude, the Christians of Wenzhou have not been terrified by threats, but have summoned the courage to face whatever God might call them to experience. As it was with the Christians in the first century, so it is with us now. In the face of persecution, courage is needed to deny evil works, to proclaim the gospel and to maintain fellowship with other Christians.

The other reason for the rapid growth of this church, and what sustained them in the midst of suffering, was the evidence of God's mighty power in miracles. During the Cultural Revolution, opportunities to preach the gospel were rare and few had the courage to take advantage of them. But in such circumstances God used miracles to bring many to faith in Christ.

Aimian reports that to his personal knowledge, demons were cast out from nine people through the prayers of Christians. "Two of these lived in my home for months and were completely delivered from demon possession. Their family, relatives and friends, even their superiors in their work unit, had tried every possible avenue for help. But both medical treatment and idol worship had failed. Then they came to ask us to pray for them. When God delivered them, those same family members and friends who had given them up as hopeless came to faith in Christ.

"In the Cultural Revolution situation, most of those who became believers had witnessed miracles in people they knew. There were, in fact, many miracles — too many for me to record. And none can be explained away by human psychology, chance or accident. They were quite evidently miracles from God, revealing the reality of His existence and power. They strengthened the faith of Christians and drew many to Himself."

To suffer with Christ is a major theme of the New Testament. Christians are destined to reign with Christ in the world to come, but they are also destined to suffer in the world now. We who live in a free and affluent society can also enjoy the privilege of sharing, in some degree, the suffering of Christ if our lives are totally yielded to Him.

SIX

THE CHURCH AMONG THE HILL TRIBES

Tony Lambert
OMF Chinese Ministries Director of Research

THE STRAINS OF HANDEL'S *Messiah* floated across the mountains and valleys from the crude, mud-brick church. The harmonies and words sounded strange to a western ear, for this Hallelujah Chorus was being sung by hundreds of Miao tribal Christians in a remote region of south-west China. The Miao Christians love to sing. Their one regret was that they only had a battered score of the music in English, a language very few of them understood. So they were delighted to receive a Chinese version of *Messiah*. Now they could sing the praises of God with even greater enthusiasm.

The five million Miao people, scattered across south-west China, are divided into many sub-groups each with its own dialect and distinctive dress. So the Black Miao differ from the Blue Miao, and these again from the Flowery Miao. Over the centuries, as the culturally more advanced Han Chinese pushed southwards, the Miao gradually retreated to the mountainous and often barren uplands of Yunnan, Guizhou and Hunan provinces. They practised primitive slash-and-burn agriculture. Despised by many Han Chinese and oppressed by tyrannical landlords and corrupt officials, their life was hard.

Early beginnings

The gospel came to these downtrodden people for the first time in the closing years of the 19th century. In 1896 Samuel Clarke of the China Inland Mission began work among the Black Miao in eastern Guizhou. Only two years later another CIM missionary and his Miao companion Pan Sheo-shan were murdered by Miao bandits. Pan was the first tribal believer in China and also the first Miao martyr — but not the last!

Christian witness to the Flowery Miao in western Guizhou began as early as 1888 when a CIM mission station was opened in Anshun. For the first fifteen years little progress was made, but in 1905 the Lord began to break through in power. Interest in the gospel spread throughout the area, and soon there were 100 church members and up to 200 attending services. Even in these early days the foreign missionaries gladly recognized that the spread of true Christianity was not so much due to their preaching as to the zeal and persistent testimony of the Miao believers themselves. This provided a solid spiritual foundation for the Miao church. Unlike many other churches in China, it was not totally reliant on missionary activity and funds, but became a largely indigenous church almost from its inception.

The Miao people are traditionally animistic. Their religion consists of placating demons and wearing amulets to ward off the evil spirits which are supposed to cause disease and death. During the mass movement to Christ in the years 1906-1908, thousands tore off their amulets and cast them into bonfires. Sorcerers' wands and drums were also burned. This showed their genuine repentance and break with their old superstitions.

Bible translation

This mass movement spread to the neighbouring province of Yunnan, where Samuel Pollard of the United Methodist Mission was also laying the foundations of a strong church among the Miao based in the city of Zhaotung. According to Pollard's biographer, this spiritual awakening "reproduced in an amazing way the phenomena of the times of the Acts of the Apostles — demoniacal possession, the appearance of pseudo-prophets, anticipation of the Parousia which caused the people in some places to give up their work so that they might be ready for the Lord's Coming, and the sending forth of (Miao) missionaries."[5] Pollard devised a new script for the Miao, who previously had no written language. He did most of the arduous linguistic work towards translating the New Testament, although he himself did not live to complete it. Eventually the entire New Testament was printed in Miao, together with hymnbooks and catechisms which greatly helped the young church.

The spreading fire

Some Flowery Miao in Wuding, north of Kunming in Yunnan, heard from their relatives in Zhaotung how they were giving up their pagan customs to worship the one True God. They pleaded with the CIM missionary Mr Nicholls to go out from Kunming to teach them

[5] Grist, *Samuel Pollard*, page 15

about Jesus. In the autumn of 1906 Nicholls established a new headquarters at Sapushan, 70 miles north of Wuding. There the local Miao built him a thatched, mud-walled house and then a chapel to accommodate 900 people. Representatives from over 50 Miao villages asked the missionary to visit them and preach the gospel.

Within a few years, thousands had heard the gospel and believed, and God raised up Miao evangelists to reach their own people. By 1909, 4,000 to 5,000 Miao in the Sapushan area had professed themselves Christians. Most of these went through two or three years of thorough Bible-based instruction.

An indigenous church

The young Miao churches in Guizhou and Yunnan were marked from the beginning by a strong emphasis on sacrificial self-support. If the tribespeople were too poor to give money, then they donated grain, chickens or other foodstuffs to the church. The secret of the survival of the Miao church in the dark days to come is to be found here in these simple, but thoroughly biblical beginnings.

By the time of the Communist victory in 1949, the Miao church in Yunnan and Guizhou was strongly established. In the Wuding area, 90% of the Miao attended the 19 CIM churches in the county. The gospel had also spread to two other tribal groups in Wuding, the Yi and the Lisu, 60% and 80% respectively of whom were Christians. In neighbouring Luquan county 60% of the Yi people professed faith in Christ — more than 8,000 believers all told. The tribal churches in Luquan had their headquarters at Salawu. There a theological college trained tribal pastors and evangelists for the ten main churches and at least 26 smaller congregations, each with its own tribal elders and deacons.

Missionaries withdraw — persecution follows

Before the CIM missionaries left, as part of the general withdrawal in 1952, Miao pastor Wang Zhiming was appointed general superintendent of all the Miao churches in the Wuding and Luquan area. However, in 1953 Communist pressure on the church increased and he was forced to work as a museum attendant. In 1959 he was labelled as a counter-revolutionary and arrested. In 1973 he was shot at the age of 65. His two sons and at least 34 Miao elders and deacons were sent to labour camps.

The tribal Christians in Yunnan suffered greatly both in the fifties and particularly during the Cultural Revolution. Some of the Lisu and Jingpo Christians who lived near the border were able to escape over the high mountain ranges into Burma where they established flourishing churches. But this option was not open to the Miao, some of whose leaders were martyred for their faith. Eventually, all the churches were closed down.

The Cultural Revolution

The Miao Christians did not dare meet during the Cultural Revolution. Their Bibles and hymnbooks were confiscated.

The experience of Little Stone Village in Wuding is typical of this period. All 70 people in the village were Christians. In the early fifties the village had gained the title of "advanced production brigade" because of the hard work of these believers. But they had little spare time for religious activities, and some became lukewarm in their faith.

In 1969 local officials forced the Christians to choose between loyalty to God or to Chairman Mao. Their leaders were tricked into going to the Communist Party headquarters, and were savagely beaten. Faced with this stark choice, the Miao Christians made their decision: they would be loyal to Jesus Christ. The authorities immediately labelled them "counter-revolutionaries" — a serious crime in Mao's China.

The authorities announced: "The land belongs to Chairman Mao. You are not allowed to use it. Nor are you allowed to keep cattle or sheep, because every blade of grass belongs to Chairman Mao!" Bereft of their leaders and reduced to dire poverty, the Miao Christians still refused to recant.

In April 1973 a vicious anti-religious campaign was launched against them and all their land was finally confiscated. Christians in neighbouring villages came secretly by night to leave food for them. But when the Party officials learned of this, they severely criticized and punished them too. In their long years of trial the Christians drew great comfort from the teaching of Scripture about Christ's Second Coming, and like their counterparts in the early church, saw suffering and the way of the cross as an integral part of the Christian life.

Anti-religious pressure

In 1976 Mao Zedong died and the notorious Gang of Four fell from power. In many areas of China the suffocating control of the "leftists" began to ease. But in the remoter parts of Yunnan extreme Maoist attitudes were entrenched. So the trials of the Miao believers were still not at an end. In March 1978 the local authorities, exasperated by the firmness of the Christians, launched yet another anti-religious campaign to "unmask the counter-revolutionaries masquerading in the guise of religion." The local peasant militia, armed with rifles and machine-guns, surrounded the village and called on the people one last time to renounce their faith and surrender. Still the Miao stood fast. So 200 militia men marched into the village and tied up every adult believer. They were dragged like animals down the mountain and thrown into prison.

The Christians cast themselves on God's Word and forgave their persecutors, saying, "We do not blame you. These things were prophesied in the Bible. All Christians must suffer persecution. The gate to Heaven is narrow. In the past we were weak in our faith. Only now are we strong!" They felt their trials even more keenly when the authorities encouraged "Christians" associated with the TSPM who had abandoned their faith to come and persuade them to abandon theirs too. Still they stood firm.

The pressures relaxed

In 1978 Deng Xiaoping returned to power and began to undo Mao's extreme policies. In 1979 the central government allowed churches to be reopened across China, and conditions improved. News of the persecution of the Miao Christians filtered through to higher levels of government. However, it was not until 1982 that high officials were sent to investigate the case. They declared that all the Miao Christians were without blame, and all were released. In the spirit of Christ, the believers refused to bring any charge against their persecutors.

Church life resumed

As political conditions eased, the Miao Christians began quietly to meet again. In Sapushan, the old CIM Miao headquarters where persecution had also been very fierce, house church meetings were resumed in 1979. In 1981 the TSPM was reconstituted in Wuding county and religious activities were allowed to come out into the open. At Christmas that year over a thousand Miao Christians met in the open air to celebrate the birth of the Saviour. In 1985 the old Sapushan church was formally reopened, and today it holds services on Tuesday, Thursday and Saturday and all day Sunday.

In neighbouring Luquan country the previous CIM headquarters for the Yi people had been taken over and used as a school. During 1983 and 1984 the tribal believers held open-air meetings which were attended by 2,000 to 3,000 Christians. They set up their own brick factory, and set to work to build a new church which was opened in August 1984. More than 6,000 Christians attended the opening thanksgiving service.

Growth

Over the last decade the Miao churches in Yunnan and Guizhou have not only returned to a degree of normality but also enjoyed much growth. In Guizhou there may be as many as 300,000 Miao Christians compared to only about 10,000 in 1949. In Yunnan, about 30,000 Miao are Christians in Wuding, and in neighbouring Luquan about 50,000 Yi, Miao and Lisu are believers compared to only 8,000 in 1949.

In the spring of 1988 a visitor met Yi believers who had come from Luquan to Kunming to attend Sunday worship. They laughed happily when he enquired about their church situation, and replied, "Oh, everyone in Luquan is a Christian!" Wuding has over 100 meeting places for worship, and Luquan over 200.

Miao church life

The simple whitewashed churches of the Miao are often perched on steep hillsides where they stand out distinctively. On Saturdays the Christians confess their sins in preparation for joyful celebration of Sunday worship. Christmas and Easter as well as traditional Chinese festivals like New Year and the Mid-Autumn Festival are seized as opportunities for large gatherings, at which the Miao believers express their love for God in song. After the long years of persecution many are hungry for the Word of God and think nothing of climbing up and down the steep valleys for miles to attend worship. A few possess tape-recorders, and eagerly record the sermon to take back to their villages.

An observer of Miao Christian communities reports that their life is their faith. The gospel has been integrated with their simple lifestyle to such an extent that there seems no sharp division between "sacred" and "secular". Their faith is expressed in gentleness of spirit and warmth of hospitality, qualities which have deeply impressed the few outsiders to visit their mountain villages in recent years.

Here the Christian faith has been handed down from generation to generation, and it is normal for whole families to turn to Christ rather than individuals. They have discarded old customs such as drinking and smoking, and in some areas are so concerned to maintain their walk with the Lord that they will not go down to the market towns to do business, for fear of developing a covetous spirit and spending less time studying the Scriptures and meeting for worship.

Problems exist

This is not to say that there are no problems. In areas where this communal Christianity is combined with a lively zeal for evangelism the church has grown and maintained its spiritual vitality. Other places, according to letters received from Miao believers, are in danger of decline into a traditional, nominal belief. Lack of leadership and of Christian literature mean that Miao Christians are also in danger of falling prey to extremes and false cults.

The educational level of the Miao is still low. According to the 1982 census 58% of all Miao people above twelve years of age were illiterate or semi-literate. This means that over half the Miao are unable to read the Scriptures, even if they had them. Only about 5,000 of a total population of over five million have had university level education.

Bibles and books

Efforts have been made, however, within China, to provide Christian books for the tribal people of Yunnan. In 1983 the Yunnan Christian Council based in Kunming began printing Bibles and hymnbooks in Miao and other tribal languages, reprinting material produced earlier by missionaries. Since then they have printed 30,000 Miao Bibles, 30,000 Miao hymnbooks and several thousand Bibles and hymnbooks in Lisu, Yi and

Lahu. Further printing is being planned.

Training leaders

In late 1988 a government-approved Bible school was opened in Kunming to train Miao and other tribal people for Christian ministry. Problems include lack of funds, as most tribal people are very poor, and also the long distances involved in travelling to the provincial capital. Because of this the TSPM has set up short-term training schools of a week or two in local centres for Miao and other tribal believers. A number of tribal pastors and elders have also been ordained.

House churches

As in other areas, the TSPM seeks to supervise and control Christian believers and to ensure that they follow Communist Party policies. Not all tribal believers are happy with this degree of political control and some are strongly opposed, seeking to worship and evangelize completely outside this state-supervised structure. Thus, alongside the officially registered churches, meeting points, pastors and elders, there exists a widespread informal network of independent house churches and evangelists.

Certain Christians run considerable risks in distributing literature received from Hong Kong to the tribal people in the mountains. Such activities have been officially prohibited in Yunnan since 1982. Occasionally Christians have had their homes searched and been detained for questioning about their "illegal" evangelistic activities.

The Miao Christians live in isolated areas still officially off-limits to western visitors and even to most Overseas Chinese. Their opportunities to obtain Christian literature other than Bibles and hymnbooks are rare and therefore some write out to Christian agencies in Hong Kong asking for Bible commentaries and other books.

Government policies for minorities

The Chinese government's policy is to tolerate the culture and religious beliefs of the minorities. So the Miao may enjoy more religious liberty today than the Han Chinese majority do. However, in some official attitudes this toleration of religious belief is associated with a somewhat patronising view of the tribal people's cultural backwardness. As their educational and scientific levels rise, religious belief is expected to wither away.

In the summer of 1988 a young Miao believer wrote to Hong Kong complaining that his middle-school teacher had derided him for his faith, openly stating that the only reason the Miao still clung to Christianity was because of their cultural backwardness. Such attitudes are a reminder that the Miao Christians, like their Han Chinese neighbours, are subject to a State ideology which is basically hostile to any religious belief.

In the long term, however, the inexorable progress of secularization and rising tide of materialism in China may prove more dangerous to Miao Christianity than official Marxist ideology has been. Hong Kong Chinese Christian visitors to the Miao Christian heartland in Yunnan and Guizhou have appreciated the deep faith and simple lifestyle of the Miao Christians. But China is rapidly changing, and the switch to a partially capitalist economy has already brought a tide of materialism sweeping across the country. Young people are consumed with the desire to get a good education and go abroad, and while moral standards have plummeted, crime rates have soared.

The Miao hidden in their mountain fastnesses have been largely immune to these trends — so far. The Miao church has survived the severe testing of persecution. Will it now be able to face this much more insidious threat, as a simple tribal culture imbued with the gospel faces the inroads of modern materialism and secularism?

SEVEN

WHERE LIVING WATERS FLOW

A western pastor

"IF THE LORD WERE to give me the choice of living in the days of the Acts of the Apostles, or in __ province today, I would choose that province!" So said the contributor of the following story, a western pastor who for the past ten years has been ministering to the house churches in Shaanxi, Henan and Shandong provinces. His ministry has primarily been to the evangelists, several hundred of whom gather for fellowship meetings. In some more general believers' meetings there may be a thousand or more present, or even as many as 4,000.

This pastor emphasizes that God is truly doing great things in China today. Words cannot possibly describe the extent of the revival and the resulting persecution. He adds that what he has witnessed is a striking testimony to the solid work of the China Inland Mission and their missionaries in this province.

There are probably over 10 million Christians in the province. In the district of L there are reported to be 100,000 Christians and in F, where the total population is 900,000, one third are believers. Most of them inevitably meet in house churches, no church buildings being available. These meetings average attendances of several dozen to several hundred.

The contributor has known those involved in the following story for ten years or more and can vouch for the factual accu-

racy of every detail. The testimony that follows was recorded on tape on March 9, 1989. The section between asterisks is translated from Brother X's own words; the later part is the testimony of the contributor.

Many different people in different districts who knew Brother X during and after his prison ordeal have testified to the accuracy of the account. Everywhere in the province he is recognized as a spiritual leader. If his story were not true, then people who have been with him for years would know this and would not accept his spiritual leadership.

*****

A dream promises healing

In our district we never heard any talk about believing in the Lord. All we knew was that there was a former Catholic church and a Protestant church long since confiscated by the government for its own use. But there were no known believers.

When I was 16 years old my father, whom I greatly respected, became seriously ill. My parents had a dream in which the Lord told them that if they believed in Jesus my father's sickness would be healed. But they did not know what "believing in Jesus" meant, and sought far and wide for someone to explain to them.

My father said to me, "Son, you must believe in Jesus. My sickness is very serious; your mother is old and your sister is quite young."

I replied, "Father, I am willing to believe in Jesus."

So when we found a Christian to explain to us that if we believed in Jesus we would receive eternal life and would go to heaven not hell when we died, I thought, That is great! Then I asked, "Is there a book about this?

Where can I get one?"

This was 1973, during the Cultural Revolution. All churches were closed and Bibles and other Christian books had been confiscated and often burned. It was dangerous to possess a Bible and the pastor who instructed our family did not want anyone to know that he still had one. So he said to me, "Child, you don't understand. The Bible comes from God and only those to whom God gives a Bible can have one. You need to pray more before the Lord." I asked, "How do I pray?"

He said, "You must pray daily before you go to sleep and when you get up in the morning. If your heart is pure and if you pray fervently and continually with tears, then the Lord will give you a Bible."

The gift of a Bible

Although I was only young and did not yet understand the ways of the Lord, I already knew that I was called to serve God. So I began to pray regularly, asking God to give me a Bible so that I could understand more of the Truth and be able to preach His Name.

We were the first family to believe in the Lord in that district. Soon all our relatives were also believing. But we had no Bibles, no song books or other Christian books to learn from.

Then I discovered a hand-copied portion of the Bible. It was already falling to pieces, but I was able to copy a few verses from it. I remember very clearly copying John 12:24, "I tell you the truth, unless a kernel of wheat falls to the ground and dies, it remains only a single seed. But if it dies, it produces many seeds." I also remember copying the verses in Matthew 16:24,25, "If anyone would come after me, he must deny himself and take up his cross and follow me. For whoever wants to save his life will lose it, but whoever loses his life for me will find it."

I read these verses over and over. I did not then understand such things as the Trinity or the Holy Spirit. I just knew about believing in Jesus. So I began to sing simple songs about believing in Jesus, and then to share what I had learned with my family and friends. That was the way the gospel spread in those dangerous times.

Still I had no complete Bible of my own. I prayed for another three months until one night I dreamed that two people came from the city bringing a large loaf of bread. I looked at it and asked, "What is this?"

They replied, "This is the Bible!"

I said, "Oh, so this is the Bible?" I accepted it and then I saw a mist which turned into a stream of water, soon becoming a rushing torrent that filled the room. I took the bread as if it was a steamed bread roll and began to eat it. As I was eating and weeping, I woke up to find it was all a dream.

It was 4 am on a cold winter morning. I got up in the dark and told my parents, "The Lord has given me a Bible." Without dressing I knelt on the floor, weeping. I prayed, "Lord, you promised to give me a Bible. Was it only a dream?"

My mother said, "Son, your longing for a Bible is so intense that you're out of your mind."

"Mother, I'm not out of my mind, I really did see two men bringing me a Bible."

Seeing how sad I looked, my parents knelt down with me and the three of us prayed for a real Bible.

As we were praying, there came a knock on the outer door and someone called my name. When I looked to see who it was, I recognized one of the men in my dream! He said that he had brought me bread from heaven. I opened the door and he presented me with a package in which was a real Bible.

Tears filled my eyes. I said, "Lord, you have answered our prayers!" I wanted to eat the Bible as I had eaten the bread roll in my dream.

The messenger told me that this was just a portion of the Bible. It was old and in poor condition. A weak brother, afraid of being caught reading the Bible, had buried it in the ground and it had become mouldy. Much of it was unusable, but some could be restored.

Memorizing Scripture

Some time later I discovered the verse in Rev 10:10, "I took the little scroll from the angel's hand and ate it. It tasted as sweet as honey in my mouth, but when I had eaten it, my stomach turned sour." This made me determined to memorize the Bible by rising early in the morning and eating only two meals a day. If I failed to memorize one or two chapters each day I would not eat my evening meal but would kneel before the Lord while continuing to memorize the Scriptures.

At that time we were very poor and could hardly afford to buy pens. Even if I had a pen, I could scarcely afford the ink. And we had little paper at home. In our village we had no electricity so, in the evenings, I would sit out in the moonlight copying Scriptures and memorizing Bible portions.

After using up what paper we had, I wanted to continue copying, so I asked the Lord what I could do. He showed me how I could write Scripture portions on my arms and legs and so be able to memorize a chapter while I worked in the fields. Each night I would wash the writing off and write another chapter. In this way I memorized the Gospel of Matthew in less than a month.

Beginning to witness

I planned to memorize the whole New Testament, but when I got halfway through Acts the Lord spoke to me in a dream. He told me, "My son, I want you to go west to preach the gospel."

I replied, "But what is the gospel?" Even though I had already memorized the Gospel of Matthew I still did not understand the gospel message.

The Lord told me again, "You are to go to a certain village to preach the gospel."

I asked, "Lord, can I do this?"

"Yes", He said, "you can."

Up to this time we had never been bold enough to hold meetings even in our own home, as this was during the Cultural Revolution when no Christian meetings were allowed.

After I memorized half the book of Acts the Lord gave me many "spiritual songs" which told the gospel story simply. My faith was very simple but strong, and the Lord gave me a great hunger and thirst for righteousness.

When the state-sponsored churches were reopened in 1980 we were delighted, and became fervent in serving the Lord. After working in the fields all day I used to go out to witness. When I was too tired to walk home I would sleep by the roadside. Many miracles accompanied our preaching. When we prayed for demon-possessed people, the demons immediately left them. When we prayed for people with serious diseases, they were instantly healed. Our practice was to witness to our relatives and friends first and, as we witnessed, miracles and signs took place.

Though we were young converts and did not know any doctrinal statements or have any teaching materials, the Holy Spirit was moving in a mighty way. The Lord did not work through the official church leaders or highly intellectual people but used unlearned people like us — as it says in Matt 21:16, "From the lips of children and infants you have ordained praise." God had given me a great love for souls and I was very fervent in my service for the Lord.

From 1979 onwards, I became a marked man with the Public Security Bureau (the police). Five or six of us preachers were constantly on the run. Whenever the TSPM found out about our activities they would report us to the PSB, who hunted us daily. We were people to be despised and cursed. On many occasions we were close to capture, but the Lord miraculously protected us.

Arrest

In 1984, while I and three fellow-workers were holding revival meetings in W county, one brother received a prophecy that within three days one of us would be arrested. That night, after the meeting had closed, the PSB surrounded the house and arrested Brother Hsu and me. We were tied up and taken away.

The Lord reminded me that He knew the suffering we were to go through, and the words of Psalm 34 came to my mind: "I will bless the Lord at all times." I also remembered how David had feigned madness when he fell into the hands of wicked men, but was delivered as he began to praise the Lord. I shared this thought with Brother Hsu and said, "From today, don't be surprised at my behaviour because, like David, I'm going to feign madness."

So, although it was freezing cold and snow lay thick on the ground, I took off my shoes. We had no overcoats. Although we were handcuffed, we began to praise the Lord during the night.

Months previously, Brother Hsu had been bitten on the hand by a rat and the poisoned arm was swollen and very painful. He could not even put on a shirt. He was prepared for imprisonment, but was afraid of the pain of being bound with ropes, a common procedure in a Communist prison. However, as soon as the guards bound him, the swelling went down, his arm was completely healed and he experienced no further pain at all.

The next day our jailers separated me from the five others who had been arrested with me. When they cross-examined me, asking where I had come from, I said that I was a citizen of heaven and when I died I would not go to hell. Then I pretended to be an idiot not knowing what to answer. When they demanded to know where our money came from I said, "From my mother."

We were all taken to the W police station and put in one empty room where we had to sleep on the floor. When we knelt to pray aloud they asked us what we were doing. "Praying that the Lord will set you free," was our answer. The room where we were detained was small, filthy and without any toilet facilities, and we were frequently beaten by the guards. As we had not been formally charged with a crime, we were forced to pay for our own food for several months before being sentenced.

On one occasion, as we were about to be beaten, one of the guards asked us why we were there.

"We are believers in Jesus and were arrested for holding a meeting."

The guard then confessed, "My mother is also a believer in Jesus, so we will not beat you this time." We spent much of our time praying and singing.

When the guards questioned us about others attending the meetings we refused to talk, despite various forms of torture, such as being prodded with electric cattle prods. We told our captors that we had been sent to prison by the Lord to preach the gospel there. And from that time on I began to witness to the other prisoners. When you are in darkness and alone it is natural to be fearful of testifying for the Lord. But the more fearful you are, the more the powers of darkness and Satan attack you. When you openly testify of the Lord, the powers of darkness flee. As I realized this, I determined to raise my voice so that the whole prison could hear my testimony.

Three periods of testimony

Our preaching band had passed through three separate periods in our evangelism. The first was when we had decided to break our silence and to proclaim Christ. Satan was defeated and for years we experienced the marvellous protection of the Lord as we went around preaching the gospel.

The second period began when a warrant was issued for our arrest. My photograph was posted everywhere and we were no longer able to associate freely with many of the brothers and sisters. So at times we felt very lonely. However, as the authorities continued to hunt for us we often experienced the power of the Holy Spirit coming upon us and we would sing passages from the Word of God to sustain our faith.

The third period, in my case, was after I had been more than three years in prison. Then the Lord led me to fast. I neither ate nor drank, and prayed for the church daily with tears.

Fasting and prayer

As I fasted and prayed, I became conscious of the power of Satan in opposition. I did not fast in order to gain merit, but to receive strength not to betray my brothers and sisters. I felt led to say nothing to my captors and to remain silent under interrogation. My prayer was for the revival of the church and that the Lord might be glorified.

For ten days I was greatly tempted to eat and drink, and then after 30 days Satan's attacks became even fiercer. The head of the jail used Scriptures such as "The servant is not above his master," and reminded me that Jesus had fasted for only 40 days. "Do you think you are greater than Jesus?" he asked. At that point I had fasted for just 38 days. I remembered John 14:12 and answered Satan with the words of Scripture, "I tell you the truth, anyone who has faith in me will do what I have been doing. He will do even greater things than these..."

In this way the Lord strengthened my determination to continue fasting and praying. Eventually, however, deep darkness enveloped me. This continued until, one evening, the Word of the Lord came to me in the words of Psalm 142:4:

> "Look to my right and see;
> no one is concerned for me.
> I have no refuge;
> no one cares for my life."

Before my imprisonment my fellow Christians had cared for me in various ways, providing food and a place to sleep, out of love and respect for me. But now that I was in prison, nobody knew where I was. I was unknown. I wept before the Lord and learned not to place my faith in others but only in Jesus. That was when I began to realize the truth that only in suffering, and as we die with Him, can we become like Jesus. If we adopt this attitude to suffering we will not become weary or discouraged.

Meanwhile, I was regarded as scum. The guards hated me more than they hated vicious criminals. They used to shut me in a filthy latrine, where other prisoners would urinate all over me. To humiliate me, they took away all my clothes except for a neck scarf. This I wrapped around me in the form of a cross, signifying that I was willing to suffer reproach and even to die as the Lord had done. I actually wanted to die and was quite prepared to do so for the Lord's sake.

After 70 days of neither eating nor drinking, I was taken to the prison hospital for a medical examination. The doctors found no sickness or disease, but were amazed to find no fluids in my body such as normal people have. And when they tried to give me an injection they could not find the vein. I was just skin and bone. The doctors expected me to die at any time.

The prison officials were aware that I had committed no crime and did not want to be accused of persecuting me to death. So they took photos and a video of me in which I was required to state that I was refusing to eat or drink of my own accord — no one was forcing me to do so.

At this dangerous crisis my only hope was the Lord. Nobody else was concerned about my situation. But, as I called on Him, I experienced anew His presence with me. I began to sing Psalm 73:25:

> "Whom have I in heaven but you?
> And being with you, I desire nothing on earth."

I also sang Psalm 123:3:

> "Have mercy on us, O Lord,
> have mercy on us,
> for we have endured much contempt.
> We have endured much ridicule from the proud,
> much contempt from the arrogant."

From Psalm 124:1 I sang,

> "If the Lord had not been on our side —
> let Israel say —
> if the Lord had not been on our side
> when men attacked us,
> when their anger flared against us,
> they would have swallowed us alive."

As I sang I began to weep, asking the Lord to hear my cry. Then the Lord came and stood before me and I clearly heard the words of Rev 3:8 "I know your deeds. See, I have placed before you an open door that no one can shut... you have kept my Word and have not denied my name."

I could hardly believe these words.

I replied: "Yes, Lord, you know my works. It is true that I have but little power, but I will keep your word and will assuredly not deny your name. Yet you say that you will give me an open door. I don't know how to believe this."

I was certainly prepared to die within days, and had even told my fellow prisoners that I would soon be leaving this world to go to be with Jesus. But these words from the Lord gave me such fresh strength and power that I stood up and began to preach to the prisoners around me, urging them to repent and believe in Jesus.

Commissioned

Weak and dehydrated as I was, I knew that the Lord had not left me. That evening, as I was kneeling in prayer, I saw three visions. The first was of a great wind (the wind of persecution) which blew all kinds of insects and scorpions (the works of the enemy) on to my body. I then saw a harlot (the false church) commanding me to run away (ie, to stop preaching), but a man in white (the Lord) told me to stand where I was (ie to continue my ministry).

In the second vision I was taken into a room in which there was white paper all around. A voice told me to put my hands on the paper as if to take my fingerprints. After I did so the paper was red with blood.

In the third vision the Lord took me outside the prison where I saw thousands lifting up their hands and praying and weeping for me. I was no longer in prison but in their midst. From that vision I received the revelation that I would eventually be released from prison — I would not die there but have a wider ministry. Later I was given to understand that the third vision spoke of the thousands of people around the world who were praying for me, even though they did not know about me.

The morning after these visions, everything began to change for me. I had already fasted for 74 days without food or liquid of any kind.[6] Some of the criminals began to come into my cell wanting to repent. They would ask me to pray for them, and an amazing change took place in their attitudes.

However, my suffering still continued, because I was still refusing to inform on my fellow believers. One of the so-called doctors came, not to treat me but to torture me. He put long needles through my finger nails into my fingers.[7] The pain was so intense that I fainted. Of course, my hands bled and this was the fulfilment of the second vision.

*****

Visitors are allowed

The prison officials then tried another device to get information out of Brother X. They allowed him some visitors, hoping that they would persuade him to talk. The first to come was Brother Hsu.[8]

---

[6] Medically speaking this is an impossibility. It must, therefore, have been a divine miracle. — Editor.

[7] I have seen the scars — Author.

[8] Brother Hsu was one of those present when we were recording this story on March 9, 1989.

Brother Hsu had seen a vision of the place where Brother X was detained, in which he was conducting Bible studies with the believers. After meeting Brother X and holding his hand, he described him as literally just skin and bone, and thought there was no way he could live much longer. He had brought a Bible with him.

On the same day, as Brother X was still refusing to say anything, the prison authorities arranged for his mother to visit him. Brother X said to his two visitors, "Have you brought the unleavened bread and the grape juice? Did you bring the body and blood of the Lord? We need to remember the death of Christ. After that I will go to be with the Lord."

They embraced him and said tearfully, "You cannot leave us. We are praying for you daily. You must stay here and serve the Lord."

However, Brother X still believed that he could not live much longer. He embraced and kissed the visitors and told them to go and assure his Christian brothers and sisters that he had not betrayed them. "I am daily praying for you too," he told them, "but I feel the Lord Jesus is calling me to my heavenly home."

The visitors begged him to take some food and drink, but Brother X refused. "My meat is to serve the Lord," he said. "Tell the church to preach the gospel. That will be food and satisfaction for me."

"Do you have a message for the church?"

"Yes, tell them not to trust in the princes or the people of the world. The rulers of the nation and the religious leaders want to destroy you."

As Brother X was speaking, the jail officials opened the door and were very surprised to find him talking.

They requested the visitors to leave. They had only been allowed in because the prisoner was thought to be on the point of death.

Brother X asked them to have the church fast and pray for him. He was now beginning to realize that the Lord might not, after all, be about to take him home to heaven, but was going to give him a ministry in the prison.

"The church will pray for you daily," they assured him. "But you must continue to live! You must continue to live!"

All this was reported to the church, which now consisted of thousands of believers in that district alone. The church fasted and prayed for days. People even stopped their farm work and other tasks to spend hours in prayer and fasting. The Scripture says in James 5:15 "The prayer of a righteous man is powerful and effective," or, as it is in the Chinese version, "produces great power." If this was the case with one righteous man, what great power must have been generated with so many righteous people united in prayer!

Miracles in healing

Now a prayer revival began to sweep through the churches of the region, and some outstanding miracles happened. The wife of a prominent government cadre was dying from an incurable disease. Having tried all the available doctors and sought help from every possible source, in desperation he took her to the Christians and asked them to pray for her. An instant miracle followed united prayer. The grateful cadre was able to arrange for Brother X's family and Christian friends to visit him in prison again.

Revival was taking place not only outside the prison but inside too! In Brother X's section there were 14 hardened criminals. After hearing the gospel from Brother X, they one by one accepted Christ. Beginning with the jailer in charge of them, they knelt to confess their sins and to trust in Christ for salvation. One factor that led them to faith was the knowledge that, medically speaking, Brother X should have been dead long ago. They saw the power and life of Christ sustaining him. Another reason was the boldness which had characterized his preaching since the Lord had appeared to him.

Brother X ends his fast

Soon after this, Brother X broke his fast and held a Communion Service with the other converted prisoners. The bread and the wine were provided by his mother and the believers outside. Now, knowing God had a ministry for him to fulfil, Brother X was full of faith and strong in body. He was continually proclaiming the gospel.

The whole atmosphere of the prison began to change. Following the conversion of the 14 criminals and their jailer, the revival spread to other parts of the prison. The converts wanted to stitch crosses on their clothes to express their new-found faith, but they had no suitable materials. So they took thread out of their hand towels, wove it into crosses and stuck them on every wall. Day and night the prison was filled with praises and hallelujahs. Prayer meetings were continually being held.

Eventually, the prisoners' behaviour and their work habits began to change, and there were no more discipline problems. The authorities recognized that this change was due entirely to Brother X's preaching and, as a kind of replay of the story of Joseph in Genesis, they put him in charge of the whole section.

New prisoners — all condemned criminals — were being admitted all the time. Brother X would welcome them and show them love in various ways. Normally the prisoner in charge is given more food than the other prisoners. But he would share his extra rations with these men. If they did something wrong, he would take the blame. As a result many accepted Christ, including a murderer. He went to his execution singing hymns and witnessing to everyone about salvation through Christ.

Due to these changes of attitude and the higher production figures, Brother X's section was given special awards and declared to be the best in the prison. It is no exaggeration to say that the prison had become a church.

Release and revival

Brother X was finally released in the early part of 1988 after a four-year imprisonment. His testimony has been heard far and wide and has greatly encouraged hundreds of other evangelists who have been arrested or are facing that possibility.

In April 1988, Brother X came to see me in Guangzhou, and in July I was invited to hold special revival meetings in his area. Brother X himself experienced a fresh filling of the Spirit at that time. The following year he arranged for a group of his fellow workers to meet me.

A few days before these meetings I happened to pass

through a district about 300 kilometers north of Brother X's district. The believers there begged me to stay for a meeting and, though I was concerned about being in time for Brother X's meetings, I agreed to do so.

The next morning Brother X and a group of his co-workers were present at the meeting! They were as surprised to see me as I was to see them. A few days previously he had been praying, when the Lord told him to travel north with his co-workers. They had no money for transport, but as they stood at the roadside praying, a northbound truck stopped, and offered them a lift. That is very unusual in today's China. The Lord led them to the very home where I was. That, too, was amazing because the believers seldom met in that home. This was an example to me of what it means to be a Spirit-filled and Spirit-led Christian.

I have attended many revival meetings and read about revivals in all parts of the world, but words cannot describe what happened at those meetings in Brother X's area. It was winter. Despite heavy snow, many travelled several hundred kilometers to attend. The power of the Holy Spirit was present in a mighty way with the gifts of the Spirit in free operation. As we prayed, virtually everyone was in tears.

The brethren regarded Brother X as having an apostolic ministry, though he himself would be the first to say "I am nothing more than God's servant." He was then only 32 years old.

Brother X had been released from prison on condition that he engage in no more preaching. The authorities of course know that he will never stop! From time to time the Public Security Bureau go to his home to check on him, but find only his wife and two sons there. Invariably they warn the wife about her husband's activities and threaten that he may find himself in prison again. However, Brother X is not afraid. He remains determined to continue preaching the gospel regardless of the consequences.

Baptisms

New churches begin weekly in Brother X's district, and hundreds are being baptized each month. Mass baptismal services are held mainly in the winter, which is safer for the preachers because there are few security police around on cold nights. Baptisms start late in the evening and often go on through to the early hours of the morning.

In November 1988 the believers cut a hole in the frozen river and began to baptize in the freezing water. On the first night 30 were baptized, and nobody complained about the cold. In fact, each emerged from the water feeling a strange, warm sensation. A 91-year-old lady who had been crippled for many years received baptism that night. Everyone was concerned about her health, but in the waters of baptism the Lord performed a miracle. As she came out she began to walk and jump like the lame man at the gate of the temple. She had been completely healed.

The news spread. The next night 60 were baptized, with similar miracles occurring. On the third night 300 were baptized, and after a few days they had to spend the whole day and night baptizing believers. In one day alone about 1,000 people were baptized, and still not one person felt the cold or suffered any ill effects.

Protection and persecution

Some young believers from Brother X's district were present in Tiananmen Square on June 4 1989. About 40 students from the same district lost their lives that day, but none of these, as far as is known, were Christians. The Christian student believers returned home with amazing testimonies to the Lord's protection.

Due to the re-emergence of the hard-line old guard after the massacre, persecution is increasing and the danger of arrest is greater than ever. However, the believers are accustomed to persecution by now and are convinced that more persecution will only result in greater revival.

The conclusion of this story must be that in China today a large segment of the Christian Church, possibly the largest segment of true believers anywhere, is living on a totally different plane from most of us Western believers. These Chinese Christians are despised by society, have no political, economic or social power or position, and materially are among the poorest in the land. Yet they are the most powerful factor influencing society. It is they who are making history. We are but babes in Christ by comparison and have much to learn from them.

The Lord has used persecution, suffering and tribulation as avenues of blessing to the church. "You have no way of comprehending this until you have personally experienced it," says Brother X. "In the darkest times we came to realize that the Lord takes the greatest pleasure in our praises. The love of God is revealed in its fullest, sweetest and most complete way in the midst of great darkness."

EIGHT

THE CHURCH IN BIG HORSE LANE[9]

Tony Lambert
OMF Chinese Ministries Director of Research

THE SOUND OF SINGING wafted down the side street. A shoe-repairer had his wares laid out on the pavement. Little girls were jumping over taut string. A couple of policemen lounged on stools in a doorway, hunched over a game of Chinese chess.

Finally I reached my destination: No.35, Big Horse Lane. A dark, nondescript doorway and a rickety flight of well-worn wooden stairs. I hesitated briefly, then went up. In the gloom I almost trampled on two young people blocking the stairway. Then I realized the whole flight was crammed with young people. Some had Bibles, others had crude mimeographed song sheets. I had come to the right address — the largest independent house church in this port city and perhaps the best known in the whole of China.

People made way in friendly fashion as I stumbled up two storeys and, blinking, found myself in a modest upper room packed with people. There must have been

---

[9] The story of this church has been published in the book **Bold as a Lamb** by Ken Anderson (Zondervan, 1991). It therefore seemed unnecessary to preserve total anonymity.

close on 200 of them squeezed together on wooden forms, balanced on the window-ledges and even lying flat on their stomachs in a narrow attic gazing down on the proceedings.

A typical service

At the front, a group of young people were playing hymns and choruses on electric guitars (rather daring, for the Church in China is conservative not only in theology but in style of worship). A large banner across the platform read "Celebrate the Resurrection of the Lord Jesus Christ — Youth Song Festival". Different groups had come to sing, play and testify to their faith. Then half a dozen tiny children went forward and acted out a drama of Jesus at the well with the woman of Samaria. I could hardly believe my eyes! Here, in Communist China where officially all evangelism among young people under eighteen is banned and where Sunday Schools are unheard of, I was eyewitness to a joyful youth meeting where the gospel was being clearly proclaimed.

The leader

The Big Horse Lane house church is no ordinary church and its leader, Brother Lamb, is no ordinary man.

Brother Lamb was born into a strong Christian family and, during the Second World War, he studied the Bible in Hong Kong. After the war he moved back to pastor the flourishing independent church in Big Horse Lane.

Following the Communist victory in 1949, dark times came for Brother Lamb. He was very friendly with Wang

Mingdao, the independent Beijing pastor universally respected by Chinese evangelicals during those difficult years. Like Wang Mingdao, he refused to join the government-controlled Three Self Patriotic Movement. When many wavered and compromised, these two men saw with remarkable discernment that the ultimate aim of the TSPM and its Communist Party masters was to neutralize the spiritual effectiveness of the Church.

Although Brother Lamb steered clear of all politics, nevertheless his straight preaching of the gospel drew the ire of the Party and their TSPM supporters. The latter were mainly liberal in their theology and more susceptible to Party propaganda, believing with many other liberal theologians worldwide that Chinese Communism was the realization of the Kingdom of Heaven on earth.

Arrest and hard labour

In 1958 the blow fell. The Big Horse Lane church was labelled a "counter-revolutionary clique" by the government and Lamb was packed off to a labour camp for twenty years of hard labour, endless indoctrination and the writing of "self-criticisms." Like countless other Christians in China, Lamb suffered for His Lord uncomplainingly. On the human level the best years of his life, when he could have been evangelizing, pastoring and training his flock, were wasted. But, like so many others, Lamb testifies that, through his suffering, he learned many spiritual lessons which now provide a firm foundation for a revived Chinese Church.

Rehabilitation

In 1979 Deng Xiaoping introduced more liberal policies and Lamb, like thousands of other "intellectuals", was "rehabilitated". He returned to Big Horse Lane to find the government had confiscated the ground floor of his home, but he was allowed to retain the first and second floors.

In prison he had kept up his English, and so was now able to give English lessons to young people eager to make their fortune as China was opening her doors to the outside world. Lamb witnessed to them, and many disillusioned with doctrinaire Maoism came to Christ. He also began to reestablish contact with older members of his original congregation. From these humble beginnings the Big Horse Lane church sprang to life again.

The dilemma

In the years 1979-1982 Lamb was able to take full advantage of the government's more liberal religious policy. In 1979 the TSPM had been resurrected and church buildings were reopened for worship all over China. However many evangelical Christians were still suspicious of TSPM intentions. Lamb had suffered at the hands of the TSPM in the fifties and saw that it was still firmly controlled by the Communist Party's United Front Work Department and the Religious Affairs Bureau — both staffed by atheists. So he was not prepared to join it. If Christ were truly the Head of His Church, how could that role be taken by the Communist Party?

Lamb, like the vast majority of Christians who choose to remain outside the TSPM, sees it as his Christian duty to obey the government and be a model citizen. But should the State encroach on the rights of Christ as

Head of the Church, then the Christian must obey Christ rather than Caesar. Lamb can and does quote China's constitution which states that every Chinese citizen has freedom of religious belief.

Growth and opposition

Armed with a clear conscience that he was doing nothing wrong in the sight of God or man, Lamb quietly built up his church. By 1982 he had a strong congregation of over a hundred members who flocked to his back-street home, conveniently situated in the centre of the city, to hear his warm expository preaching. Two worship services were held each Sunday. On Tuesdays there was a prayer and testimony meeting and on Thursdays an evangelistic outreach meeting to which Christians were encouraged to bring their relatives, neighbours and friends. From the end of 1981, Lamb held a young people's meeting every Friday evening. Many of the educated youth of the city were drawn in and were led to faith in Christ.

The city authorities and the TSPM were not at all pleased. This vigorous manifestation of biblical Christianity in the very heart of the city was completely outside their control! In December 1982 they acted.

The local TSPM issued a secret instruction to its officially registered church workers, saying that Lamb was carrying out "illegal activities". He was accused of printing Christian books and copying and distributing Christian tapes illegally[10]. In an astonishing piece of Orwellian Newspeak the TSPM stated, "Forbidding

---

[10] In China all publishing is controlled by the State and consequently there is a dearth of Christian literature.

Pastor Lamb's illegal activities is a powerful measure taken by the government to uphold normal religious activities. We will fully implement this correct expression of the policy of freedom of religious belief."

Lamb was urged to "reform" himself and join with "patriotic" Christians who had accepted TSPM control: "The doors of the two city Christian organizations [TSPM and the China Christian Council] are wide open, welcoming everyone, even those who have made mistakes, to change their attitudes and return to the one big family which loves country and loves religion," he was told. Such is the reality of "freedom of religious belief" in Mainland China. Lamb could only bow to the storm and he temporarily suspended all his public meetings.

In 1983 China was swept by a ferocious Communist Party campaign against "spiritual pollution". This meant any ideology, especially the growing influences from the west, which conflicted with Marxist orthodoxy. Although Christians were not the chief target, they suffered indirectly and many throughout the country were arrested. Whenever the Chinese Communist party adopts a leftward doctrinaire stance, the Church always suffers, either directly or indirectly. It is regarded at the best of times as a marginal group with a suspect ideology.

Lamb knew that this was not the time to confront the State. Christians were still able to meet in small groups in their homes and such cell meetings were a highly effective form of evangelism.

Bursting at the seams
By early 1984 the full vigour of the "anti-spiritual pollu-

tion" campaign had subsided. Lamb quietly began to build up his house church again. By 1985 the church was more flourishing than ever.

Over the next four years over 1,300 people — many of them young — were baptized and 700 to 800 were regularly attending services in this back-street dwelling. Improvements were made in the fabric: the leaking roof was completely replaced; electric fans were installed to ease the hot, humid southern summer atmosphere; and a loud-speaker system allowed an overflow meeting on the first floor to share in the services.

Despite these modifications, it was quite impossible for everyone to cram inside the building at the same time. No more than 250 people could possibly attend any one meeting. So Lamb introduced a system whereby he preached the same sermon three times in the week — on Sundays, Tuesdays and Saturdays! This encouraged cohesion among the Christians.

Training others

Lamb was very aware that he could not himself undertake all the ministry. In recent years he has been training a team of six co-workers, who are all totally reliant on the freewill offerings of the congregation for their livelihood. In a Communist society where it is axiomatic that everyone in the cities has a regular occupation and receives government ration cards for basic commodities, these dedicated young people have indeed taken a great step of faith.

An international fellowship

News of the work of the Big Horse Lane house church has spread far and wide. Brother Lamb has welcomed

Christian visitors from all parts of the globe — Hong Kong, USA, Britain, Australia, Canada, Japan and many other countries. In 1988 Dr Billy Graham visited Big Horse Lane and spoke briefly to a packed-out meeting.

This free expression of international Christian fellowship is very unusual in China. In the TSPM-controlled church, foreign visitors are usually processed through official channels. Most independent house churches are very low-key and avoid foreign contacts as too dangerous. Factors in the unique freedom enjoyed by the Big Horse Lane congregation may include its proximity to Hong Kong, the fame of Brother Lamb's ministry among Hong Kong and Overseas Chinese, and his wisdom in cultivating western contacts over the years.

Fresh pressures

However, such freedom is fragile at the best of times. After five years of relative liberty to develop the Christian ministry, Brother Lamb again came under strong pressure from the local authorities in the latter part of 1988. New provincial religious regulations drawn up by the People's Government earlier that year called for strict registration of all Christian congregations and required their affiliation with the TSPM.

In August 1988 Brother Lamb was summoned to a police station and interrogated. Five further summons followed. On each occasion the police, sometimes backed up by the Party Religious Affairs Bureau and TSPM officials, put strong pressure on him to register and join the TSPM. They even offered him the use of the largest church building in the city! Some of the arguments they used were ingenious: for instance, if

Joseph, Mary and Jesus were registered at Bethlehem with the Roman authorities, why should Big Horse Lane resist registration with the Chinese government?

On each occasion Brother Lamb courteously declined, and quoted the Chinese constitution in support of the Christians' right to meet for worship without joining the "patriotic" church. He even turned the tables on them, stating that although he had once had the chance to leave China he had never taken this up, unlike certain "patriotic" church pastors who eagerly used every opportunity to send their children overseas to study and then encouraged them to stay there! True patriotism, in Lamb's view, was more than mouthing political slogans. Rather, Christians by their honesty, hard work and example were demonstrating their love for their country in actual deeds. On this score, Big Horse Lane had nothing to be ashamed of.

Lamb knew from long experience that as soon as he joined the TSPM, subtle pressures would gradually be brought to bear, and many of the church's thriving ministries would inevitably wither.

Students for democracy

By early January 1989, the city authorities had eased their pressure. But the Tiananmen massacre in June that year led to fresh control over every sector of society, including the Church.

Brother Lamb, like most independent house church leaders, chose to remain uninvolved in the democracy movement. Whatever the private feelings of Christians attending the Big Horse Lane church, Lamb knew that political involvement of any kind would be suicidal for house church believers. Suspect as they are at the best of times and harrassed by an atheistic government, any open show of support for the student movement would bring down the wrath of the hard-line authorities.

As several members at Big Horse Lane said, "Even in ordinary times the authorities are looking for opportunities to give us trouble. If now, in connection with the student movement, we are perceived to do something wrong, no matter how trivial, we are sure that they will take immediate action against us." Another member stated, "The work of the Church is the spreading of the gospel. The Church is not a political body. As a rule, Christians are to be obedient to those who govern, as Paul advised in Romans 13."

The Big Horse Lane Christians believe firmly in the priority of evangelism and the need to address the root of social problems by preaching the gospel which alone can change man's sinful, selfish heart. They do not place their hopes in political reform. As one Christian stated: "The fact is that no government is perfect. The overthrow of one government and the establishment of another does not solve the problem of sin. Dynasties come and go, but sin remains. We should not expect too much from human politics."

The priority of evangelism

To evangelical Christians overseas, who are beginning to grapple with the whole problem of the Christian's involvement in political and social issues, such views may sound pietistic. However, faced with the stark reality of political and religious repression in Communist China, the Church has only been able to survive by a complete disengagement from political activism. In a society traumatized by endless political campaigns, purges and sloganizing, the simple preaching of the gospel of repentance and faith in Jesus Christ comes across with amazing freshness and power. That is why, in many parts of China, the Church is experiencing unprecedented growth.

The story of the Big Horse Lane congregation, despite its unique features, is only one small part of an ongoing revival movement which is gathering force. The crushing of the student movement in 1989 brought many Chinese intellectuals and young people to the brink of despair. As a result many turned to Christ. China today, although suffering under political repression, is a ripe harvest field.

Like an occupying army

In early 1990 Brother Lamb felt the repercussions of the new hard-line policies in Beijing directly. On the evening of February 22, more than 50 policemen burst up the stairs and arrested him. In Pastor Lamb's own words, "It was like an occupying army!" He described his harrowing experience as follows:

"All the Christian books, the Bibles from overseas, several thousands of our stencilled tracts and 3,000 copies of our hymn books were confiscated. They then took me away and interrogated me for 21 hours. I only slept for ten minutes all this time. They said we had disobeyed Document 44 of the Guangdong Provincial Government and so were suppressing our Big Horse Lane meeting-point."

Brother Lamb vigorously denied suggestions that his church was dependent on overseas funds and that his acceptance of Christian books from overseas was "imperialist infiltration." He argued reasonably with his persecutors. "Why do you call this 'infiltration' when you call the entry of science, technology, English and overseas literature 'cultural exchange'?" Lamb even shared the Gospel of John with his persecutors. "If I did not believe that Jesus truly rose from the dead when I was first arrested (in the fifties) I would have discarded this dead Jesus. But after I was arrested twice, my faith was not only strengthened, but I proclaimed the Risen Christ because it is true."

Finally, at 4 am on February 24, Pastor Lamb was released. However, the government forbad the church from meeting and pasted a notice to that effect on the front door. The next Sunday, many Christians came as usual, but were not allowed to enter. People stood out in the street to pray. Some wept.

The irrepressible Brother Lamb

The arrest of Brother Lamb was a clear signal from the hardline government that henceforth independent house church activity would not be tolerated. The shock waves were felt by the house church community throughout China, and overseas among Chinese Christians, especially in Hong Kong. However, the amazing fact is that despite this prohibition, by the late summer of 1990 the meetings at Big Horse Lane had quietly started up again and as many, if not more, people were attending services throughout the week. Brother Lamb seems quite irrepressible. Nevertheless, he was clearly walking on very thin ice. By the end of 1990 the authorities had summoned him for "discussions" more than half a dozen times.

The authorities, in fact, seemed to be playing a game of cat and mouse. In the first part of 1991, the pressures eased. But in October, Brother Lamb was again warned by the police that he must register his house church or close down. The full weight of the communist system was brought to bear: in the space of a few weeks, Pastor Lamb was visited by the police and 13 members of the Municipal People's Congress. It was even reported that the Army were involved, and discussed his case at one of their conferences. Before Christmas, Brother Lamb was warned by the TSPM that his meeting would be closed down. But Christmas came and went without incident. He received similar warnings before New Year 1992 and Chinese New Year (February 1992) but nothing happened. Under this pressure, Brother Lamb told a Hong Kong visitor in early 1992 that he and his co-workers were ready to go to prison at any time.

As Brother Lamb's ministry and the pressure he is working under have become more widely known, Christians across the world continue to lift him, and the Big Horse Lane church, to God in prayer. If he were to be imprisoned again, and the church permanently closed, the Chinese government could face an international outcry.

Uncertainty, pressure — even persecution — have been part of everyday life for Christians at Big Horse Lane over the past forty years. Only one thing is certain — come what may, Brother Lamb and his congregation will continue to spread the Gospel of Jesus Christ among their countrymen by every possible means.

CAUSES OF CHURCH GROWTH

The growth of the Church in China has truly been phenomenal. It is almost impossible to grasp the magnitude of what God has done and is still doing. But this raises two questions.

Why was church growth before the Communist Revolution so slow?

1. The association of Christianity with imperialism, since the Opium War of 1840, was a major stumbling block. Dr Sun Yat Sen took up the theme in *The Three People's Principles* and the Communists have never ceased to tar the Church with the imperialism of the missionaries.

2. China's proud Confucian culture, held to be far superior to Christianity, was a formidable barrier to the progress of the gospel.

3. Other factors include the huge size of China, the relative lack of travel facilities in the nineteenth century, and the high mortality rate among missionaries before the days of modern prophylactics. The great diversity of languages continued to be a major hindrance to effective missionary penetration.

How can we account for the amazing growth of the Church since the end of the missionary era?

1. Missionary foundations
Credit must first be given to the missionaries who sowed the Good Seed and planted the churches in the 110 years prior to the Communist takeover. They nurtured the plants well. Growth was certainly slow, but the Church was well-rooted and grounded. The building (to change the metaphor) had solid foundations in a biblical faith.

So the fierce persecutions from 1951 onwards, and especially during the Cultural Revolution, failed to destroy the Church. On the contrary, it discovered its reserves of strength and came through the ordeal purified and strengthened. Many who had been trained before the Revolution in missionary theological and Bible colleges are now preaching and teaching in present-day theological colleges, or pastoring the new churches.

2. Revival
Three times in this century the Church in China has experienced the cleansing, renewing fire of revival. Each appears to have been a clear preparation for suffering and trial: the first Revolution and anti-Christian agitation (1911-1921), the Sino-Japanese war and the suffering it entailed (1937-45), and the Communist Revolution for which the post-war revival, especially among students, was a preparation (1949 on).

3. Changed lives
The Chinese people were deeply impressed by the witness of the Church under persecution. The Christians'

patience under trial, their practical love for one another and compassion for the needy both outside and inside the Church, did not go unobserved. People saw their good works and were prepared to give glory to God. The changed lives of believers and their sacrifical lifestyle are speaking volumes to a spiritually hungry nation.

4. A failed ideology

The disastrous Cultural Revolution seems to have destroyed any confidence there may once have been in the philosophy of Marx and Lenin and in the Thoughts of Mao. The youth of China are politically perplexed and seeking an alternative to these beliefs — real democracy, genuine freedom, but, above all, truth. "China," says Paul Kauffman, "is in the vacuum of a lost faith and is now more ready for a spiritual awakening than it has ever been in its long history. There is a hunger for a faith beyond the grasp of the state."[11]

A neighbourhood Party boss remarked to a tourist in the presence of a BBC correspondent, "You don't know it, but Christianity is spreading rapidly in China because people are disillusioned with Communism." Letters to the Far East Broadcasting Company (FEBC) express deep discontent and wistful longing. The Revolution may have met the basic needs of the people, but the very materialistic nature of government policies has left an aching void, a hunger in the heart. Today Jesus, through His disciples, is supplying the multitudes with the living bread as literally and as simply as He did in Palestine.

[11] Asian Outreach

But a generation brought up to believe that all religion is superstition will be hard to convince about the basic truths of the Christian faith. 200,000 or so selected Chinese students are currently studying abroad and their presence in the USA, UK and elsewhere provides opportunities to demonstrate to them that Jesus Christ is the Way, the Truth and the Life.

5. Radio broadcasts

In 1977, restrictions on listening to foreign broadcasts were lifted (although subsequently reimposed), and the mail response to FEBC's broadcasts shot up. In the first four months of 1978 about 6,000 letters were received, most from non-Christians. Correspondents were scattered in all parts of China, even the most remote. During 1980 FEBC received 9,320 letters, many from new believers appealing for Bibles and Christian literature. In 1986 10,136 letters were received. Letters are still flooding in, providing abundant evidence that the truth of the gospel is reaching people all over China and appealing to their need.

These Christian stations have sustained Christian faith through the dark years and brought countless people to faith. Radio is the one way the gospel can reach every creature — at least everyone who owns a transistor radio, and that would include most of the population of China.

6. The death principle

A major reason for the growth of the Chinese Church is the principle Jesus set out in John 12:24: "Unless a grain of wheat falls into the ground and dies, it remains alone; but if it dies, it bears much fruit." What was true of the Lord Himself became the pattern of fruitful Christian witness for all time.

Ever since the Communist revolution in 1949, the Church has had to endure bitter suffering and grievous loss. Many of the Church's leaders have spent twenty years or more in prison or exile, separated from their families and Christian friends and often without a Bible. To this day, house church leaders and evangelists are hounded, arrested and imprisoned without trial.

Chinese Christians have come to regard suffering as a glorious privilege to be desired, not avoided. They interpret the last forty years of prolonged suffering as a gift of God's grace to purify the Church in preparation for future fruitful service. So many grains of wheat have been going through the ordeal of death that, out of the soil of China, a harvest which still today cannot be estimated is springing up.

7. *The power of prayer*

The Chinese Church has always been a praying Church. From the earliest days, Christians learned about the power of prayer. In a country where demon possession was widespread, early Christians like Pastor Hsi Sheng-mo[12] whose name meant "conqueror of demons" proved the power of the Name of Jesus to exorcise demons. Demon possession is still very common in rural areas. Evil spirits trouble new and untaught believers, who sometimes make prophetic or other strange utterances through them. Thus a young believer may imagine himself to be some sort of prophet and expect people to follow him and even to

---

[12] See *Pastor Hsi*, Mrs Howard Taylor, OMF Books

pray to God in his name.

Where there were few medical facilities, the only resort for Christians in times of sickness was to prayer. And prayer for healing was answered times without number. Ever since the 1949 Revolution, which showed itself firmly opposed to the miraculous, miracles of healing have continued to be a powerful witness to the Living God. They have convinced even Party members, who have themselves been healed. Whole villages are known to have turned to Christ after seeing the evidence of His miraculous supernatural healing power. Chinese Christians all say that the main reason for the present growth of the Church is believing prayer.

8. *Evangelism*

From its earliest beginnings the Christian Church in China was taught the obligation and the privilege of witness. The short history of the Church includes the work of many outstanding evangelists. The Bethel Bands went all over China in the 1930s, leaving behind scores of voluntary local bands committed to evangelism. Similar bands inspired by Dr John Sung, the great evangelist-scholar, can still be found witnessing in parts of South-East Asia. Evangelism was a Chinese tradition. And today, in spite of formidable difficulties and strong opposition from the authorities, fruitful evangelism is taking place on an unprecedented scale, and a huge harvest is being gathered in.

9. *Indigenization*

Indigenization was the ideal of the early pioneer missionaries in the 19th century. It was urgently pressed on the churches after the first Communist uprising in

1925. Missionaries taught the churches the principles of self-support, self-government and self-propagation and showed themselves willing to relinquish their own authority. Many churches successfully achieved independent status before the 1937 Sino-Japanese war, and proved the wisdom of those principles during the long years of war and the troubled peace which followed.

Without any doubt, the Church today is thoroughly Chinese. The roots put down in Chinese soil a hundred years ago have been going deeper over the years. Before 1951, although the Church was free from western domination, its culture and ethos were still conditioned by the west. Now this also has changed. According to Bishop K H Ding, "The stigma of being a western religion has been pretty much removed."

Forty years have gone by since the formation of the TSPM. The present generation has never seen missionaries and now accepts the Christian Church as a national "people's movement". The Church today knows no dependence on foreign support or direction. It has lost its "foreign image" and is attracting new members in very large numbers.

10. *The work of God*

Some Christians in Henan province were asked why there had been such an enormous increase in the number of believers. They replied, "At one time, because of persecution, the fire of the gospel was almost extinguished. But then the Spirit of God took the seed which had been sown in the midst of suffering, and fertilized it so that it has brought forth this great harvest. Christians have become a mighty army!" What is happening to the Church in China, therefore, is the direct result of God's sovereign activity and the mighty power of His Holy Spirit. "God really is among us," one leader declared, "and the time is ripe for Him to reveal His glory!"

APPENDIX

SUMMARY OF CHURCH GROWTH AROUND CHINA

Fujian and Zhejiang

The greatest church growth has taken place in the two coastal provinces of Fujian and Zhejiang where the Church first took root in the nineteenth century, and in the inland provinces of Henan and Anhui. Reports of church growth in Fujian have already been recorded (see page 9). North from Fujian is Zhejiang, where inland Protestant missionary work first began. Hudson Taylor and his first party of pioneers settled in Hangzhou, the beautiful lakeside provincial capital. Officially there are 900,000 Christians in the province meeting in 1,600 churches, but with only 300 pastors. When the 140,000 Roman Catholics are added in, Christians form one quarter of the population!

In Hangzhou alone there are three churches and 700 additional meeting points. The Drum Tower Church holds three services each Sunday attended by about 3,000 people. Two-thirds of the members have become Christians during or since the Cultural Revolution. Eighty baptisms on a single day is not uncommon.

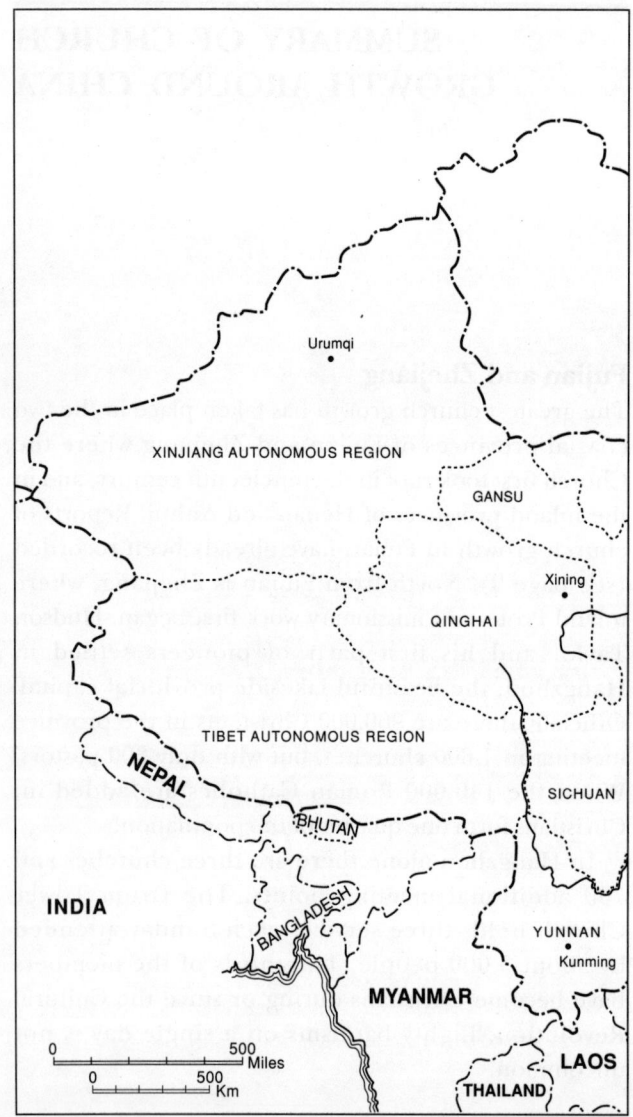

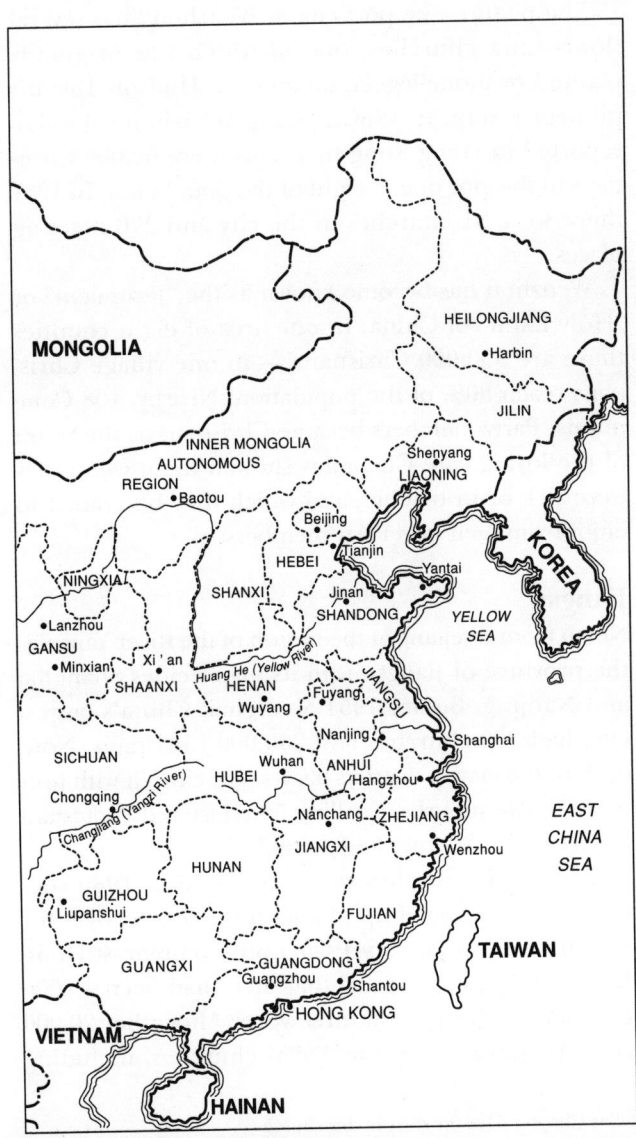

The picturesque port city of Wenzhou[13] has several flourishing churches, one of which was originally planted by a one-legged member of Hudson Taylor's pioneer group. In 1980 a young Wenzhou Christian reported in Hong Kong that there were 50,000 Christians in the city, one in eight of the population. In 1981 there were 31 churches in the city and 270 meeting places.

Wenzhou has become known as the "Jerusalem" or "Holy Land" of China. In one area of eight counties there are 330,000 Christians — in one village Christians reach 80% of the population! Nearby, 108 Communist Party members became Christians as the result of the loving care Christians showed them when they were sick or in trouble, and which they had failed to enjoy from their own Party members.

Jiangsu

North from Zhejiang at the mouth of the River Yangzi is the province of Jiangsu with its major cities Shanghai and Nanjing. Before 1951 Shanghai, China's largest city, had 200 churches and 200,000 Christians. Now, each of the eleven districts has its own church with four more in the suburbs, totalling 55 registered Protestant churches and 30 "meeting points".

When the churches were reopened in 1980 very large crowds queued up to attend the first services for fifteen years. In January 1990 a pro-Communist Hong Kong newspaper reported that there had been 15,000 baptisms in Shanghai in three years. Altogether 20,000 converts have joined the TSPM churches, including

---

[13] See Chapter 5 for the story of this church.

many "intellectuals", young people, professors, doctors, engineers, authors and students.

The total TSPM membership is about 40,000, but to this must be added the literally hundreds of house churches in this huge city. Itinerant preachers teaching the Word in Zhejiang and Jiangsu cannot begin to meet the great need of new believers.

In the last ten years the Protestant Church has grown to 70,000 to 80,000 Christians, which includes some diehard old Party members. According to TSPM figures, the number of Christians in the province grew from 250,000 in 1985 to 300,000 in 1987 — a 20% increase in two years!

Jiangxi

From Shanghai travellers have long followed the great River Yangzi to the west. First on the south bank is the mountainous province of Jiangxi. Here Mao Zedong established the first Chinese "soviet" in 1928. The churches have suffered much persecution, but now "vast numbers" are said to be turning to the Lord. A visitor found 5,000 to 6,000 believers in four large villages. One small city has up to 120,000 believers and another town 70,000. The TSPM church in Nanchang baptized 1,000 people in two years. Half the new converts are middle school graduates. In one place, as many as 2,000 Christians hold their meetings on the deserted highway at night to sing, pray and listen to visiting preachers.

Anhui

On the north bank opposite Jiangxi is the province of Anhui, once a notorious Maoist stronghold. Even before the revolution the church experienced unusual growth there, and in recent years 75,000 people have turned to Christ. The TSPM reports that the church in Anhui now numbers 800,000, a twentyfold increase on the pre-Liberation figure.

In Fuyang in the north of the province, 1,000 attend the TSPM church, while in the surrounding countryside about 200,000 Christians meet in house churches. In Fuyang alone there are 350 house church evangelists, most of them young people with limited education, who meet regularly for planning, prayer and fasting. Bibles are still in short supply and the churches are threatened with false teaching and division. Christians have also suffered much at the hands of the local authorities and the TSPM.

In another medium-sized city which had only eight believers in 1982, the church had grown to over 1,000 by 1986. In three neighbouring counties 70,000 believers are meeting in 50 centres.

Hunan

Pursuing our way up the river, we reach the province of Hunan on the south bank — Chairman Mao's native province and the last one to hold out against Christianity in the 19th century. In one county with a population of 200,000, church membership grew from 7,000 in 1949 to 50,000 in 1989. In some communes Christians are numbered in thousands and even tens of thousands. The official membership figure is 60,000.

Hubei

On the north bank is the province of Hubei with its large conurbation of Wuhan, including the famous port city of Hankou. Again, in some communes Christians are numbered in thousands, and the official figure for the province is 80,000.

Sichuan

Leaving Hankou, river steamers continue their journey through the spectacular Yangzi gorges to Chongqing in Sichuan. Sichuan suffered severely during the Cultural Revolution and the church has been tightly controlled. Growth has been slower than elsewhere. The TSPM has only 60 churches and 100 meeting points with a membership of 500,000. But in north Sichuan, through the labours of a house church evangelist, believers in five counties increased from 30,000 to 50,000.

Qinghai

Travelling north-west from Sichuan we reach Qinghai, bordering on Tibet. The province is named after the huge salt lake which dominates the high, bleak plateau. Once it was populated by roving Tibetans, but today many Han Chinese have moved in, attracted by the rich mineral deposits. The province also has the sinister reputation of being China's gulag for political exiles. In 1950 Xining, the capital, had only 120 Christians, now there are at least 3,000.

In the early 1980s three ageing pastors were released from labour camp where they had endured great suffering, and returned to their homes in Xining. The chapel which had been used as a jewellery factory was returned to the Christians in 1981. Soon a group of twenty women began meeting for prayer, though the memory of severe persecution was fresh in their minds. Their faith was rewarded. Numbers grew rapidly to 3,000, the converts including a handful from Islam and a dozen former Party members. Altogether in the province there are probably 15,000 Christians, few of whom however are Tibetan or Hui.

Ningxia

Ningxia is an autonomous region, the population being mainly Muslim. Even here there are at least 10,000 Christians.

Gansu

Gansu, west of Ningxia, was once regarded as among the poorest of provinces. But now Lanzhou, the capital, which bestrides the Yellow River, is China's second industrial city with 90,000 Christians. The total Christian population of the province is 260,000, which would surprise the early pioneer missionaries who thought of it as a barren mission field. The main church in Lanzhou, seating 800, is always overcrowded on Sundays, and there are many "meeting places" besides. Between 1981 and 1985 nine baptismal services were held in which a total of 1543 were baptized, a third of them young people. In May 1989, 270 were baptized. Plans are in hand to build a church seating over 2,000 with three or four floors.

Travellers report a mighty revival under way in the province. In Minxian county, 10,000 believers meet in 14 "meeting points", but they lack Bibles and pastors. There are also known to be 200 Tibetan Christians in South Gansu.

Xinjiang

Taking the Shanghai-Urumqi train from Lanzhou we

travel through the Gobi desert to Urumqi (Dihwafu), capital city of what was once known as Chinese Turkestan. It is inhabited by minority groups like the Uighurs and Kazhaks, though many Han Chinese have migrated there in recent years. Where missionaries once toiled almost in vain, the 24 counties of this Autonomous Uighur Republic now have as many as 15,000 believers. A Trans World Radio report says that Xinjiang is the fourth most responsive province to radio broadcasts.

Urumqi itself has 1,500 believers in one main church and twelve household churches for Han Chris-tians. Alas, there are none among the six million Muslim Uighurs, the one million Kazhaks or the 13 other minority nationalities. But how Mildred Cable, George Hunter, Percy Mather and others would have rejoiced to see this day!

Inner Mongolia

Between China and the former USSR is the vast area of Mongolia — Inner Mongolia, under the Chinese and the small People's Republic of Mongolia, formerly under Soviet influence. This, too was a difficult and unresponsive field with its nomad people devoted to Buddhism. But, even here in Inner Mongolia, one area has twelve household groups of about 80 Christians in each. There are 20,000 Christians in Baotou, according to Bridge magazine. "The work of God is prospering among the Han Chinese, but few Mongols are turning to Christ."

However in the People's Republic, where ten years ago there were no believers, more than a score of believers are meeting in two congregations, and the

New Testament is available in Mongolian.

Manchuria

The north-eastern provinces of China (Manchuria) once experienced widespread revival. Now the church there is also recovering from the years of persecution. In one small town nearly 500 converts were registered in three or four years. In another town close to the Soviet frontier there are 2,000 or 3,000 Christians, and over 120 were baptized in one year. The Wen Hui newspaper reports 140,000 Christians in Heilongjiang and 30,000 in Jilin. There are 2,000 believers in Harbin, and the TSPM church in Liaoning has grown from 150 to 400. In Shenyang, 25% of the 6,000 believers are young people. One miracle of divine supply led to a whole village turning to Christ. 10,000 Korean Christians also live in Manchuria.

Hebei

Coming to the Yellow River basin, we find two provinces to the north of the river and two to the south. Hebei ("north of the river") contains Beijing, the national capital and Tianjin, the port city. Beijing suffered greatly in the Cultural Revolution and Christianity has been slow to re-emerge. But two well-attended Protestant churches have been opened and also the Catholic cathedral. There are known to be a number of house churches in and around the city. But the capital has been one of the hardest places in which to maintain a Christian witness in recent years.

Officially there are 72,500 Christians in the province but as in other cases the official figures do not include the large numbers of believers in the house churches.

Shanxi

Shanxi, the province in the great bend of the Yellow River which is known as "the cradle of Chinese civilization", has Christian churches everywhere. This province suffered greatly in the Boxer uprising of 1900, but also experienced revival in the 1930s. "An innumerable number of people are coming to Christ," said one report. In north Shanxi as many as 3,000 people believed through listening to radio broadcasts. In another area two old believers started to witness to such effect that a church of several thousand grew up, with a hundred workers. *Tian Feng*, the official church newspaper, reports 40,000 believers in all in 14 meeting points.

Shaanxi

Crossing the Yellow River westward we arrive in Shaanxi with its population of 30 million. Xi'an, the capital, was the ancient imperial city where Christianity first appeared in China in the seventh century. Nestorian Christians were then given the emperor's permission to build a church and a seminary. Now Xi'an has several reopened churches and at least 70 household churches attended by 30,000 believers. In all there are 50-60,000 believers and 500 to 600 fulltime workers.

In one village one whole section of the commune turned to Christ because of the witness of a 60-year-old lady. Even the commune officials began to read the Bible and to support Christian activities.

A visiting preacher found Christians in 89 villages in south Shaanxi, with over 100 believers meeting in each place. A November 1989 report told how, because the rate of conversions was so great, one church was restricted by the government to two baptismal services a year and 100 believers at each service. Protestant Christians in the province number at least 180,000 officially, but a 1984 report from the RAB regretted that only 2% of those baptized since since 1981 had been baptized in the TSPM church in Xi'an.

Henan

East of Shaanxi is Henan ("south of the river"), the province which has witnessed the most prolific church growth of all. There the church has multiplied many times, due overwhelmingly to the grassroots house church Christians.

In 1949, when the missionaries withdrew, fewer than 100,000 believers lived in the province. Now, it has 600,000 registered believers and 200,000 enquirers — with only 80 pastors. There are also 2,200 independent house meetings and 500 independent churches. Most villages in Henan now have house churches.

The 70 reopened church buildings are quite inadequate to accommodate all the Christians and many gather in the "meeting points". The government has returned seven buildings to the Christians, and eight new churches have been built. *Tian Feng* lists 41 registered churches. But it is the house churches that have seen such phenomenal growth. One county alone has 30,000 Christians, two thirds of them young people. There are said to be 100,000 believers in each of 15 counties. The official newspaper, *China Daily*, has reported the great growth of Christianity in Central Henan, where more than 10,000 were meeting in one county and 100,000 in another.

The area of Wuyang has seen a great revival, with the number of Christians increasing from 1,000 in 1949 to

15,000 today. Every village has a meeting point. One well-known pastor, Xu Yongzi, leads 3,500 independent churches and tens of thousands of believers. He was arrested in 1988 while on his way to meet Billy Graham, but was released in 1991.

This one province today has more believers than the whole of China in 1949![14] Such figures would stagger pre-1951 missionaries! But even the figure of one million Christians in Henan may be far short of reality.

It is also encouraging to hear one pastor report that 10,000 young people wish to serve God full time: they are very zealous, but, so far, insufficiently trained. Hundreds of evangelists already trained have been sent out from provinces like Henan and Zhejiang to the remotest parts of China.

Shandong

The Yellow River flows down through the golden loess soil of north China to the sea through Shandong, once famous for its silk, and the scene of stirring revivals in the 30's. It is still witnessing strong and remarkable church growth and house meetings are multiplying. In Jinan, the provincial capital, it is reported that there are 20,000 Christians. Yantai (Chefoo), the port city and former home of the CIM school, has six churches, 45 meeting points and 4,800 registered believers. The official figure for the province's Christian believers is 250,000.

Yunnan

The mountain ranges of south-west China have been

[14] Christians in China in 1949 estimated at 700,000

home to many hill tribes, driven there over the centuries as the Han Chinese gradually occupied China's fertile eastern half and drove the tribes out. In Yunnan and Guizhou, the "national minorities", as they are officially designated, number 600,000. Before the Communist revolution, many of the tribes responded warmly to the gospel and large, flourishing churches were established.

Today, 95% of the 800,000 registered Christians in Yunnan, and an equal number of unregistered Christians, belong to the minorities. The number of tribal Christians has multiplied tenfold during the past thirty years and now stands at half a million. This includes probably 180,000 Lisu Christians, 30,000 Wa and 25,000 Bai Christians. Miao and Yi each number 150,000. The government is considering recognizing Christianity as the official religion of the Lisu. Nearly every Lisu village has a church. In Salawu, the church membership has grown from 300 to 6,000 Yi believers.

In 1986 a delegate conference of the Christian churches in Yunnan was held in Kunming, the capital. 103 delegates representing eight tribes together with the Han Chinese attended. It was reported that, during the previous five years, 20,000 people had been baptized and many meeting points opened. 35 pastors had been ordained and 80,000 Bibles distributed. At Easter 1989 200 were baptized in Trinity Church in Kunming, which is always packed with 300 to 400 worshippers.

Guizhou

Guizhou, a notoriously poor, mountainous province with a population of 30 million, is also home to many tribes, 300,000 of whom are Miao (see chapter 6 for the story of the Miao church). In 1986 14 Miao pastors, 26 elders and 27 preachers were ordained at Gobu, which indicates a healthy, growing church. In May 1990 500 Christians crammed into one church where 80 were awaiting baptism. In the Liupanshui region of north Guizhou there are 6,000 Miao and Yi Christians. Christians in the whole province number 300,000, compared with 10,000 before 1949.

Guangxi

Further east from Guizhou is another rugged province, home to the largest minority group in China — the Zhuang who number 13 million. Of the 12,000 Christians among them, 2,000 have been baptized since 1981. 71 Han churches which closed down during the Cultural Revolution have now been reopened for worship for 7,000 Christians. In addition, there may be as many as 3,000 house churches in the province. Officially the province has 40,000 believers.

Guangdong

Further east still is the populous province of Guangdong whose capital is Canton (Guangzhou). Canton has four churches attended by 2,700 each Sunday. There have been 930 baptisms since 1980. Canton also has 60 house churches. Pastor Lamb's "Big Horse Lane" church is perhaps the best-known house church in China, with 500 members. Pastor Lamb has baptized 500 people over the past seven years (see chapter 8).

The port city of Swatow (Shantou), north of Canton, has three churches with 764 registered Christians and a total of 10,000, of whom 300 to 400 attend weekly Bible classes. In addition, there are many unregistered meetings. Officially there are 130,000 Christians in the province.

Hainan

Hainan is an island off the south coast of Guangdong, famous for producing good cooks. The church is growing apace here, too, after a wave of persecution in the 50s and 60s. There are many house churches, some with an attendance of 350.

Summary

In statistics released in 1987, world statistician David Barrett said surveys indicated that China had a total of 4,000 churches and 81,600 worship centres, with 21,500,000 baptized adult believers and a total Christian community of 52,152,000. In 1991 new believers are said to be joining the Church at the rate of 100,000 per annum!

BIBLIOGRAPHY

Adeney, David; *China: The Church's Long March* (OMF Books and Regal Books, 1985)

Broomhall, AJ; *Hudson Taylor and China's Open Century*, 7 volumes (Hodder & Stoughton and OMF Books, 1981-1989)

Lambert, Tony; *The Resurrection of the Chinese Church* (Hodder & Stoughton and OMF Books, 1991)

Latourette, Kenneth Scott; *A History of Christian Missions in China* (SPCK 1929)

Lyall, Leslie T; *A Passion for the Impossible* (Hodder & Stoughton, 1965)

John Sung, Flame for God (CIM 1954)

Mac Gillivray, Donald; *A Century of Protestant Missions in China* (1967)

Steer, Roger; *J Hudson Taylor, A Man in Christ* (OMF Books 1990)